ATIONAL PARK (ZION CANYON SECTION)

Potato Hollow

THE NARROWS

RIVER

VIRGIN

WEST CANYON

ORDERVILLE CANYON

Mountain
of Mystery
1995 m
6545 ft

Temple
of Sinawava
1344 m
4411 ft

Observation
Point
1984 m
6508 ft

Angels
Landing
1763 m
5785 ft

Cable Mtn
1980 m
6496 ft

THE GREAT
WHITE THRONE
2056 m
6744 ft

Grotto

Hidden Canyon

Lady Mtn
2115 m
6940 ft

ZION
LODGE

THREE PATRIARCHS

Court of the Patriarchs

Deertrap Mtn

CANYON

WHITE CLIFFS

1912 m
6273 ft

EAST
ENTRANCE

Mountain
of the Sun
2049 m
6723 ft

The
Sentinel
2181 m
7157 ft

Checkerboard Mesa

TOWERS OF THE VIRGIN

Altar of
Sacrifice
2259 m
7410 ft

The
Beehives
2077 m
6825 ft

The East
Temple
2167 m
7110 ft

The
Great Arch

TUNNEL

Canyon Overlook

2033 m
6670 ft

ZION

Bridge
Mtn
2076 m
6814 ft

TUNNEL

1562 m
5124 ft

The West
Temple
2376 m
7795 ft

SOUTH
ENTRANCE

Springdale
1185 m
3887 ft

NORTH FORK

The Watchman
1998 m
6555 ft

VIRGIN

PARUNUWEAP CANYON

RIVER

EAST FORK

kville

Legend:

Paved Road	
Gravel, Dirt Road	
Trail	
Parking	
Self-guiding Nature Trail	
Amphitheater	
Ranger Station	
Picnic Area	
Lodging	
Campground	

0   1   2   4   6
KILOMETERS

0   1   2   4
MILES

Plants of Zion National Park

PLANTS OF ZION NATIONAL PARK &

Wildflowers, Trees, Shrubs and Ferns

by Ruth Ashton Nelson

with drawings by Tom Blaue

ZION NATURAL HISTORY ASSOCIATION

International Standard Book Number 0–915630–00–1

International Standard Book Number 0–915630–01–X (pbk.)

Library of Congress Catalog Card Number 74–28958

Zion Natural History Association
Zion National Park, Springdale, Utah 84767

Printed in the United States of America by Deseret Press

Designed by Robert Jacobson

Contents

Foreword

THE PROSPECT of another handbook about Western wildflowers by Ruth Ashton Nelson is indeed a delightful one, especially to those many people who have enjoyed her other scholarly, informative, as well as intimate handbooks on Rocky Mountain flowers. For over four decades, *Plants of Rocky Mountain National Park* has enabled people in North Central Colorado to become better informed about the vascular plant cover of that area. Those who have been privileged to use this handbook develop the feeling they have spent hours, even days, in the field with Ruth Nelson as their guide.

As one who has had the special privilege to walk many trails of Rocky Mountain National Park with Ruth Nelson, I have seen firsthand the close coincidence between the person in real life and the botanist-author that shines through the written page. This woman has a deep affection for, devotion to, and comprehension of the land and its diverse plant cover. For her, collecting plants and making observations about their habits and habitats is not a coldly mechanical undertaking. She loves life in all its forms. She has strong affinity for the land that is life's dwelling place. She expresses profound quiet reverence for the natural world through everything she says and does. This is a rare and valuable trait in a profession where a premium often is placed on being objective, sometimes to the exclusion of being human or showing any warmth.

Mrs. Nelson is highly qualified for preparing this new plant handbook for Zion National Park. Not only has she had extensive formal university training in botany, but she has studied and collected plants in the field up and down the Rocky Mountain chain from Canada to Mexico, as well as in the Canadian Rockies and the Alaska Range. Much of this work was in tandem with her renowned botanist husband Dr. Aven Nelson, who founded the Rocky Mountain Herbarium at the University of Wyoming, and who taught botany at that institution from nearly its inception.

It is a distinct professional honor and with great personal pleasure that I take this small part in the *Plants of Zion National Park*. We are all the richer having known Ruth Ashton Nelson—personally and through her writings.

12 February 1975

BEATRICE E. WILLARD, Ph.D.
Member
Council on Environmental Quality
Washington, D.C.

Introduction

THIS BOOK has been written for the visitor to Zion National Park who wants to learn to recognize the Park's wildflowers and other plants. An attempt has been made to keep the book simple but accurate. All of the plants known to exist in the Park are included. Most are described in the text, and many are illustrated either in color or by drawings. Some inconspicuous plants not of interest to the general public, such as the majority of grasses and many of the introduced plants, are simply listed and not described, but their names are included.

The technical or Latin name of each plant is given in secondary place so that all who are sufficiently interested may look these plants up in more technical botanical books on the region.

Latin names in parentheses are synonyms or names which have been commonly used for the species in earlier books. In order to save space authorities for the Latin names have not been included but may be found in the reference books listed.

How to use this book

THE TEXT CONTAINS simple, informal keys to groups and usually to species, based for the most part on easily observed characteristics. The author believes that those who make an effort to use the keys will find it rewarding because it encourages close observation of the plant characteristics, and gives a more thorough understanding of each individual species. It also helps one to learn to recognize the features which indicate plant relationships, thus increasing one's general knowledge of plants.

Descriptions are given for each family, and in most cases for each genus. Anyone seeking to identify a plant should read these descriptions because the general information given in them applies to each species in the group and is not always repeated in the specific description. Also some of the technical terms used in the specific descriptions are defined there. In addition all technical terms used in the book are defined and often illustrated in the glossary. Dictionaries are good sources of information for botanical terms.

In using the keys to identify plants, the reader will find two or more coordinate statements in each category. At first it is helpful to read all the statements in each category. Compare them and then compare the plant you are trying to identify in all details with these statements. Choose the one which most nearly describes it. This may lead you to a plant family or a group of families, or it may lead you to another pair or group of coordinate statements. Follow in this way until you come to a specific name. Then check the individual description. If your plant does not fit the description, observe more carefully looking up terms you might not understand. Then try again. If there are two possibilities, check each one. The more plants you work with the easier it will become to identify species by this method.

Keys are not always satisfactory. To provide for all the exceptions and variations inherent in living plants would have made the keys too cumbersome to be of any value. I hope that their usefulness in many cases will outweigh their imperfections and possible omissions in some particular instances.

Where there are more than one species in a genus, the generic name is given in the generic description or for the first species described. In succeeding descriptions only the initial letter of the generic name is given with the specific name. The names of all illustrated plants have been assigned a number. This number is used in each place where this particular plant is mentioned. The numbers are arranged consecutively.

An attempt has been made to use everyday words in so far as possible, but it is often impossible to describe a plant briefly without the use of some botanical terms. These have been kept to the minimum consistent with accuracy and clarity. Names of over 700 kinds of plants are included.

Common names for plants cannot be standardized because if they are to be meaningful they must have grown out of the folklore of the region. The same name is applied to different plants in different areas. Interest in the plants of our region is too new to have permitted the application and general acceptance of many folklore names. Consequently, in this book, in the absence of a generally accepted common name adaptations of the Latin botanical names, such as translations or the generic name with a descriptive adjective, have often been used. The authority for the Latin names and for common names where given is, in most cases, the *Checklist of the Vascular Plants of the Intermountain Region* by Arthur H. Holmgren and James L. Reveal, because it is the only publication which specifically pertains to the plants of southwestern Utah.

For readers who wish a quick color reference to the most frequently seen kinds of plants, a short section on "Common Roadside Flowers by Season and Color" may be found on page 298.

The keys and descriptions have been made to apply particularly to the species which occur in Zion National Park. The book will be useful over a much larger area but some details given may not always apply to plants outside this region.

ALLEN HAGOOD

FIGURE I. *View of Zion Canyon showing all types of vegetation from the river to the canyon rim.*

Vegetational Zones and Habitats

OUT OF THE soft, colorful Navajo sandstone in southwestern Utah the Virgin River has carved a beautiful canyon. At this time in geological history its floor is relatively flat, about one half mile wide, and the almost perpendicular walls are one thousand to fifteen hundred feet high. Around their rim stand domes, spires and isolated tabletops of pink or buff sandstone. This is Zion Canyon (fig. I). The river enters the canyon from a very narrow gorge (fig. II) and, after a comparatively quiet passage of about fifteen miles, flows out into the broader arable Virgin Valley.

This is semi-desert country. The precipitation in the canyon is only about fourteen inches per year. Most comes from summer thunder showers, often locally violent ones; about a third of the total falls as snow during the early months of the year. The soil, worn down by wind and water from the sandstone walls, is loose, unstable and rocky. These conditions impose severe restrictions on the plant life of the area. The loose soil, the dry air and the long hot summers eliminate moisture-loving plants except in some specialized spring-fed areas and right along the stream bed. Fremont cottonwood is the dominant tree in the river bank vegetation (fig. III).

The plant species found here are adapted in different ways to the exacting habitat. Many are perennial plants with more or less woody stems and deep or long roots. The annuals are mostly short season

7

plants which germinate following the early spring rains, bloom quickly so that some seed is matured even if the season is unfavorably dry, and then wither away. In exceptionally dry years the seeds of some annuals may lie dormant throughout the whole season, as desert plants often do, waiting for more favorable conditions.

There is seldom a dense cover of vegetation. Plants are spaced to take advantage of the available moisture. See foreground, fig. I. Little annuals often spring up in the semi-shade afforded by shrubs. Many plants are thorny or tough in texture. Some have very small leaves; others have their leaf edges curled inward, a feature which reduces the surface exposed to evaporation; some are covered with hairs which insulate them from the drying atmosphere.

FIGURE II. *A view of the lower end of the Gateway to the Narrows where the Virgin River emerges into Zion Canyon.*

FIGURE III. *The Virgin River and riverbank vegetation.*

VICTOR JACKSON

The type of native vegetation of any area is determined by the growing conditions. These include temperature, amount of available moisture, soil conditions, and exposure to sun or shade and to air movement in the form of wind. In the overall picture, temperature seems to be the primary determining factor in plant distribution. Altitude affects the average temperature. An increase of 1,000 feet in altitude equals a decrease of approximately three degrees in average temperature.

Natural scientists have given names to the types of vegetation characteristic of particular climatic zones. These zones are defined in relation to altitude, and they correspond roughly to belts of latitude across the continent. In Zion National Park there are three such zones. Within each zone the character of plant life varies with local conditions of

FIGURE IV. *Lower Sonoran Zone view showing desert type shrubs with Fremont cottonwood along a stream bed.*

FIGURE V. *Hanging gardens become established on wet-faced cliffs and seepage areas.*

moisture, exposure and topography so that the zone is not a clearly defined belt sharply differentiated from the ones below and above it. It is, rather, an area in which certain characteristic plants dominate the scene and give it a distinctive appearance.

We recognize the Lower Sonoran Zone by the presence of creosote bush, blackbrush (88) and salt bush (51). Besides desert-type shrubs the Fremont cottonwood occurs here along the water courses (fig. IV). In general this zone includes the area below 4,000 feet. It exists in only a small portion of the Park at the lowest elevations, particularly Coalpits Wash, the Parunuweap, and the area along the Watchman Trail. The Lower Sonoran vegetation may extend upwards on open, south-facing slopes, just as the Upper Sonoran vegetation extends downwards in shaded canyons and on north-facing slopes. Moisture also affects the distribution, and plants normally of higher elevations may be found at low situations around seeps and along water courses.

One of the most interesting plant communities in this semi-desert region is that which occurs around springs and seepage areas. These springy places usually develop under protecting overhanging lips of

10

FIGURE VI. *Much exposed sandstone surface called slickrock is dotted with hardy shrubs, especially littleleaf mountain-mahogany (94). Their roots penetrate crevices in the rock.*

FIGURE VII. *Field of sand sagebrush with pinyons.*

harder strata as at the Weeping Rock. In such places the plant life is luxuriant. Great banks of maidenhair fern (4) occur along crevices, clumps of pink-flowered shooting star (136), scarlet monkey flower (164) and cliff columbine (60) flourish along with violets, star-flowered solomon plume (25) and giant helleborine orchid (34). The contrast between these lush hanging gardens (fig. V) and the desert type vegetation of the dry canyon wall or the slickrock (fig. VI) intensifies one's interest in both.

The Upper Sonoran, from roughly 4,000 feet to about 5,500 feet is characterized by the pygmy forest of Utah juniper (14) and pinyon (11). It includes yuccas (26, 27), Gambel oak (37), Utah serviceberry (89), singleleaf ash (137), littleleaf mountain mahogany (95) and princesplume (69). Most of the canyon is included in this zone. Some-

12

FIGURE VIII. *Mature ponderosa pines on the East Zion Plateau.*

times on benches or gentle slopes at edges of the pinyon forest considerable areas are covered with the fine-textured silvery sand sage (fig.
VII). In the cool side canyons we find the oaks growing into small
trees. Also bigtooth maple (114) and numerous shade-loving wildflowers occur there.

Above this on the plateaus at from 5,500 to 7,500 feet is the Transition Zone characterized by ponderosa pine (10) (fig. VIII), Douglas
fir (13), white fir and Rocky Mountain juniper (15) (fig. IX). Figure I
also shows this zone as a mantle of evergreen forest on top of the
highest plateaus. The moist glades of this forest have a very different
character than the lower rocky slopes and provide a habitat for mois-
ture- and shade-loving plants (fig. X).

References to localities are, in most cases, self-explanatory, being the

13

FIGURE IX. *Hanging coniferous forest of the Transition Zone.*

FIGURE X. *Purple penstemon in mountain forest.*

terms commonly used by the Park personnel for specific areas. One exception may be the use of East Zion Plateau for the region along both sides of the East Entrance road, the Mount Carmel Road. This area is frequently cited, and since it did not seem to have a specific name, the author adopted the one given above.

ALLEN HAGOO

FIGURE XI. *Cottonwood and salt cedar, autumn.*

Blooming Seasons

BLOOMING STARTS in late winter. On the warm sandy benches and lower plateaus the little clustered buds of manzanita (135) may begin to open their jug-shaped bells in February. Sand buttercups (63) with white and pink blossoms come soon afterwards. By early March the Zion milkvetch (103) shows up as purple patches on the west-facing banks along Zion Canyon Scenic Drive. Soon yellow parsley (132), pink or white phlox (142) and rich red paintbrush (161) become noticeable. In an unusually cold and late spring the timing may be two to four weeks later.

Then the whole array of spring and early summer bloom follows until the heat and drouth of mid-June slow down the procession and leave only a few heat-resistant kinds to decorate the trails and slopes. These are mostly white-flowering night-blooming species like the datura (159) and evening-primroses (126).

But with the heat come thunder showers which moisten the dry ground, and in September a second blooming season begins. At this time numerous plants of the composite family come into flower, many of them with yellow blossoms. So there is a new show for this season which lasts into October. Add to this the glorious autumn coloring of the bigtooth maples in late October, and the bright golden dress of the cottonwoods (fig. XI) which lasts well into November, and the colorful plant cycle has come almost full circle.

17

On the high plateaus spring arrives much later. Not until late April or May do the earliest flowers appear. Here this season extends through the summer and ends in mid-September when frost and snow check visible activity.

FIGURE XII. *Ample snow in Zion Canyon ensures abundant wildflowers.*

18

Plants of Zion National Park

with keys for their identification

Informal Key to Main Groups

greenish, reddish, white or yellow. Some are rarely noticed, but many in the buckwheat and four o'clock families are conspicuous. See illustrations, numbers 41 to 53.   78

2. Petals separate and individual flowers usually conspicuous, flower parts usually in 4's or 5's.

   A. Petals 4, ovary superior (see glossary p. 312)

                         Mustard and **Caper Families** 112, 124

   B. Petals 4, ovary inferior (see glossary p. 314)

                              Evening-primrose Family 180

   C. Petals usually 5.

      1. Ovaries superior, see family descriptions 100

      2. Ovaries inferior.

         a. Stems succulent, petals many   **Cactus Family** 174

         b. Stems not succulent, leaves stick to clothing

                              Blazing-star Family 172

3. Petals united and flowers usually conspicuous.

   A. Flowers gathered into a compact head surrounded by an involucre (see glossary illustrations p. 319)

                              Composite Family 250

   B. Flowers in various types of inflorescences but not as above.

      1. Plant families with corollas regular.

         a. Ovaries superior 192

         b. Ovaries inferior 244

      2. Plant families with corollas irregular.

         a. Ovaries superior 218

         b. Ovaries inferior 250

These plants differ from flowering plants in being more simple in structure and in their reproductive processes. Reproduction is by spores, tiny bodies which are produced in large numbers in specialized structures and particular locations.

SPIKEMOSS FAMILY, *Selaginellaceae*

These are moss-like plants less than an inch tall. They have firmer stems and are more substantial than true mosses. Their leaves are very small, triangular or awl-shaped, and crowded on the intricately intertwined, creeping stems. Their reproductive spores are in tiny orange spheres borne in the leaf axils, barely visible to the naked eye. These plants grow on loose dry sand or on rock surfaces and are important, along with lichens, in building up soil in which seed plants can begin to establish themselves. Two kinds are known in Zion National Park:

Underwood spikemoss, *Selaginella underwoodii*, is a loose-growing, trailing plant, usually found on rocks.

Utah or **Zion spikemoss,** S. *utahensis*, is a more dense and compact plant. The latter was first described from specimens collected on Lady Mountain in the Park. It occurs in other locations in the Park and in the Charleston Mountains of southeastern Nevada.

HORSETAIL OR SCOURINGRUSH FAMILY, *Equisetaceae*

These are plants of poor, usually wet soil. The stems are hollow, green and jointed; leaves are reduced to small triangular teeth which occur around the stem at its joints. The plant tissues contain silica particles which give them an abrasive quality which accounts for the name scouringrush. The fruiting bodies are small, brown or straw-colored, cone-like structures borne at the tips of the stems. The spore cases occur under little umbrella-like protuberances on the surface of the cone. Three species occur here:

Common horsetail, *Equisetum arvense*, is a very widely distributed plant. Its vegetative stems have many whorls of slender drooping branches which suggest a horse's tail. The fertile stems are brownish,

23

parasitic on the green plant, and appear very early in the spring, usually before the green stems develop. This plant often becomes common on poor soil such as the cinders of railroad banks.

1. **Common scouringrush,** *E. hyemale,* has evergreen, usually unbranched stems which may be 3 or 4 feet tall, usually banded with black or gray at the joints where the small pointed leaves make a sheath around the stem. Its cones are sharp-pointed.

2. **Smooth scouringrush,** *E. laevigatum,* is similar, but the sheaths tend to widen upwards and its cones are rounded. Both occur at the edges of streams and on wet ground.

FERN FAMILY, *Polypodiaceae*

The majority of ferns are plants of moist, shaded situations, but there is a group in semi-desert areas which, through evolution, has developed adaptations permitting the species to survive in very dry locations. The leaves of these plants are often firm, tough in texture, their divisions reduced in size and their surfaces clothed with hairs or scales. New leaves may appear at any time when moisture is available. They often curl as they dry, to uncurl again at a time of more moisture. These are some of the characteristics which reduce evaporation and permit these plants to survive drouth.

Zion National Park has some of the species which live in cool, shaded canyons where moisture is plentiful and some which grow in dry rock crevices and under ledges on dry hillsides.

Fern leaves rise from creeping underground rootstocks, often in clumps or banks, but sometimes singly and scattered. Each consists of a stalk and a blade. The stalk extends through the blade to its tip and is called the *rachis*. This rachis may or may not be branched. The leaflets arranged along either side of the rachis are called *pinnae*. They may be variously shaped, divided or toothed around the margin.

Reproduction is by spores, tiny bodies which occur in specialized structures and in particular locations. These structures, called *sori*, are usually on the under or back side of the pinnae. In most cases the sori are protected until ready for spore dispersal by small thin coverings.

FIGURE 1. Common scouring rush,
stems green

FIGURE 2. Smooth scouring rush,
stems green   SCALE: 1 x 1

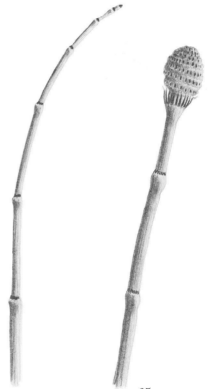

25

The shape and position of the sori and coverings are important in identification. Some species have the sori continuous along the margins and others along margins which are inrolled. Still other species have sori at the tips of the leaflets with a tiny tooth of the leaf margin turned back over them. Perhaps because of the lightness of the spores, which can easily be carried by air currents or water, the kinds of ferns are very widely distributed throughout the world.

I. Ferns with stalks and rachises dark brown or black.

A. Stalks and leaf surfaces smooth.

3. **Little ebony spleenwort,** *Asplenium resiliens,* has narrow, clustered, evergreen leaves, 4 to 12 inches long; it is a rare fern of moist, shaded situations in rock crevices.

Black spleenwort, *A. adiantum-nigrum,* is another rare, delicate fern. Its leaves are about 4 to 10 inches long, the blade elongated-triangular in shape, the pinnae finely cut and lacy, usually dark on the underside due to spreading and merging of the sori. This species is widely distributed in Europe, Asia and Africa as well as in South America, but is known to grow only in three locations in North America, near Boulder, Colorado, one place in northern Arizona and Zion National Park.

4. **Southern maidenhair,** *Adiantum capillus-veneris,* is one of the most abundant ferns in Zion, occurring around springs and along seepage lines on moist cliffs. It is especially profuse at Weeping Rock. Its main stalk is often more or less zigzag.

FIGURE 3. Little ebony spleenwort
SCALE: 1 x ½

FIGURE 4. Southern maidenhair
SCALE: 1 x ½

27

5. **Birdfoot maidenhair,** A. *pedatum,* which is much rarer, occurs in moist, cool canyons. Each stalk in a well-developed leaf divides into two rachises, and each of these divides again into two or more long slender pinnae. Stems of the maidenhair ferns were used by the Indians to make black patterns in their basketry.

Goldfern, *Pityrogramma triangularis,* is a small, very rare plant in the Park. It grows in dry rock crevices of pinyon-juniper and ponderosa pine areas. The leaf has three main divisions, and its lower side is covered with a yellowish powder.

Cliffbrake, *Pellaea.* These are ferns of dry rock crevices with brittle, dark brown or purplish stalks twice or thrice pinnate, and oblong or roundish leaflets. There are tufts of long thin scales at the bases of the stalks.

6. **Spiny cliffbrake,** *P. truncata,* has little spines at the tip of each leaflet and a dark stripe through the center of each basal scale.

Purple cliffbrake, *P. glabella,* is similar but lacks the dark stripes and the spines at the leaf tips.

B. Stalks and leaf surfaces with hairs or scales, the smallest leaf divisions tiny, bead-like.

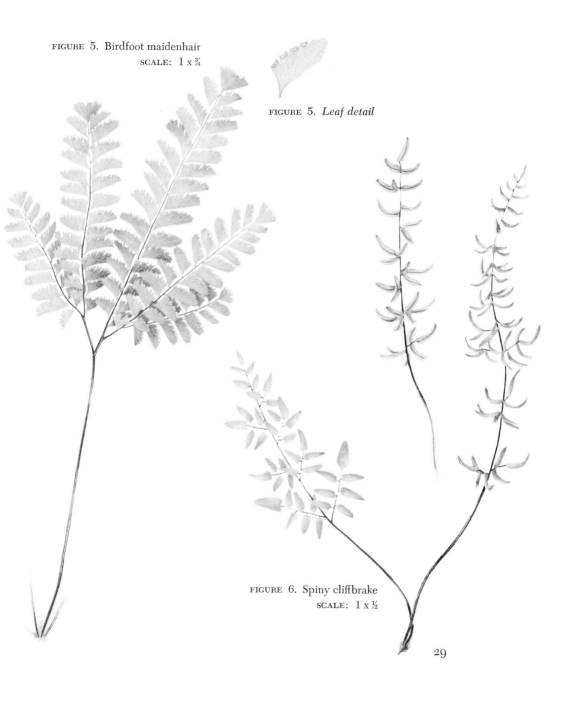

FIGURE 5. Birdfoot maidenhair
SCALE: 1 x ¾

FIGURE 5. *Leaf detail*

FIGURE 6. Spiny cliffbrake
SCALE: 1 x ½

7. **Slender lipfern,** *Cheilanthes feei,* has hairs on both the leaf surfaces and on the stalks. **Coville lipfern,** *C. covillei,* has the upper surface smooth but many thin, long-pointed scales on the under surface. Both these lipferns grow on usually shaded but dry rocks and in crevices or under ledges in rather dry areas. The leaves with their stalks may be about 5 to 10 inches long.

 II. Ferns with stalks and rachises green or light brown.

  A. Pinnae divided or cut.

 Bladderferns, *Cystopteris.* These are delicate lacy ferns of moist, shaded situations. Leaves are thin, veiny and usually wither early when weather becomes hot. **Brittle bladderfern,** *C. fragilis,* is the most commonly seen. It is widely distributed throughout the northern hemisphere. It varies in size depending on moisture and soil conditions; leaves are usually from 4 to 10 inches long, tapering at the tip. **Bulblet bladderfern,** *C. bulbifera,* is similar though larger and coarser and much less common. It usually has 2 or 3 bulblets on the underside of the leaf.

 Bracken, *Pteridium aquilinum pubescens,* a stout coarse fern of dry or moist slopes, often in woods, with long-triangular leaves which may stand up to 3 feet or more tall. This has underground, spreading rootstocks so the leaves appear scattered, often over large areas. After frost the leaves turn a bright orange brown.

FIGURE 7. *Leaf detail*

30

FIGURE 7. Slender lipfern,
ultimate leaf divisions bead-like
SCALE: 1 x 1

31

8. **Male fern,** *Dryopteris filix-mas,* has its leaves in clusters, several from a central crown. They may be from 8 inches to 3 feet long, tapering more at the tip than at the base. Conspicuous on the underside are the round sori which contain the spores.

B. Pinnae undivided but may be toothed.

Western hollyfern, *Polystichum scopulinum,* is another rare fern in Zion with evergreen, leathery leaves. There are brown scales along the lower part of the stalk, and the pinnae are sharply toothed. Leaves are up to a foot or 15 inches long.

9. **Western polypody,** *Polypodium hesperium (P. vulgare),* is a crevice fern with a running rootstock from which leaves arise at intervals. The leaflet margins are nearly smooth; leaves are from 3 to 10 inches long. Its sori are without covers and often appear as bright orange-brown, round spots. This fern is widely distributed in the northern hemisphere. In the Park it will be found on dry rocks of shaded canyon sides.

FIGURE 8. Male fern

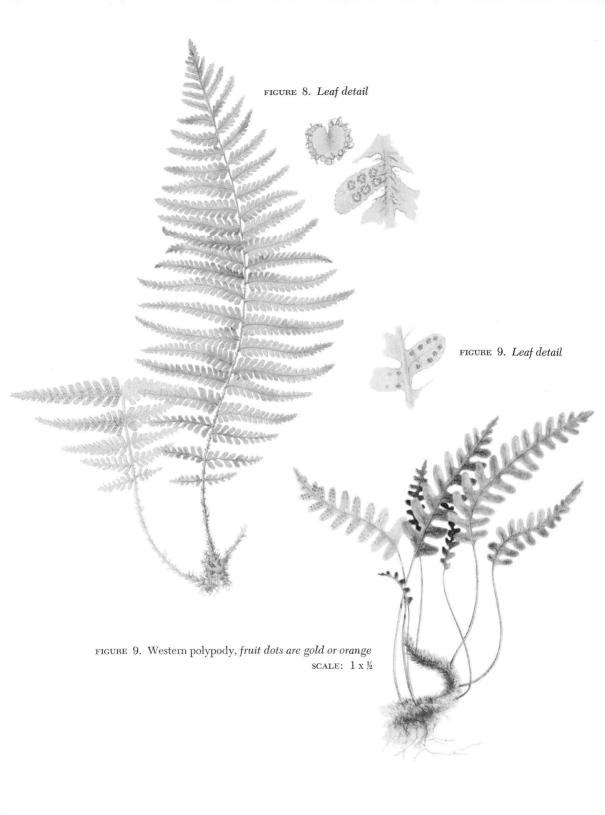

FIGURE 8. *Leaf detail*

FIGURE 9. *Leaf detail*

FIGURE 9. Western polypody, *fruit dots are gold or orange*
SCALE: 1 x ½

CONEBEARERS, JUNIPERS AND JOINT-FIRS (Gymnosperms)

This group includes three families in this region: pine family, cypress (juniper) family and joint-fir family. This group is distinguished from the flowering plants (Angiosperms) by having its seeds uncovered and borne on scales which are arranged in cone-like structures.

PINE FAMILY, *Pinaceae*

> I. Leaves needle-like, in bundles of 1 to 3, each bundle surrounded by a short, thin sheath. Cones are firm and woody, maturing at the end of the second season . . . **Pine,** *pinus*

10. **Ponderosa pine,** *Pinus ponderosa,* is the largest tree in the Park. In this region mature trees may be up to 70 feet tall and 2 to 3 feet in diameter with a more or less flat top and rough orange-brown bark. Needles are in bundles of 2 or 3, about 4 to 6 inches long. Younger trees have blackish bark and are not flat-topped. Cones are brown, 3 to 6 inches long. This tree is common on all the plateaus and comes down almost to the main canyon floor in a few places in shaded side canyons. It is the most important lumber tree of the region. Before the area was made a national park, logs for millions of board feet were brought down from the East Rim Plateau by way of the old cable on Cable Mountain.

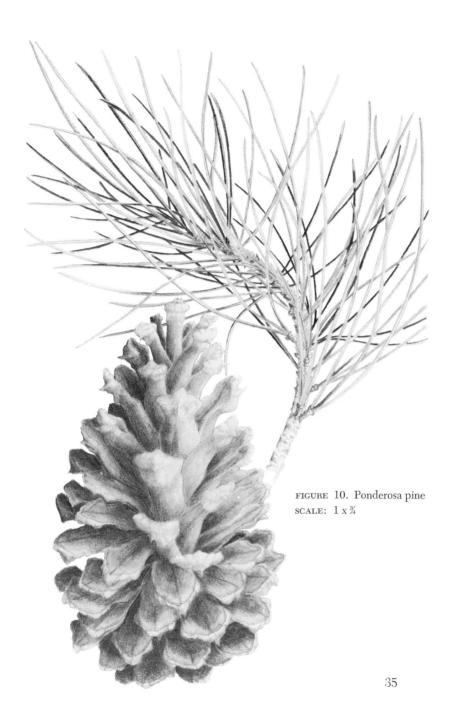

FIGURE 10. Ponderosa pine
SCALE: 1 x ¾

11. **Pinyon** or **nut pine,** *P. edulis,* is the common pine of the dry slopes around Zion Canyon which often intermingles with ponderosa on the lower plateaus. It has a bushy shape, black bark and 2 bluish-green needles in a bundle.

12. **Singleleaf pinyon,** *P. monophylla,* which is almost as common and similar in appearance, has the leaf bundle reduced to one needle. Cones of both are short and without prickles. At Zion National Park the ranges of these two trees overlap; the first extends eastward to southern Colorado and New Mexico, where it is the state tree; the second is abundant in Nevada where it is the state tree. They are both commonly associated with the Utah juniper (14), but the pinyons extend to higher elevations. Together they form the Pinyon-Juniper Woodland which covers many square miles of the arid Southwest. Nuts of *P. edulis* are preferred, but both are still used extensively for food by the Indians.

   II. Leaves needle-like, never in bundles but attached singly to the branch, usually less than 2 inches long; cones with papery or cartilaginous scales, maturing at the end of the first season.

13. **Douglas fir,** *Pseudotsuga menziesii,* has flat needles about 1 inch long. Cones are pendant with 3-pronged bracts which protrude from

FIGURE 11. Pinyon
SCALE: 1 x ¾

FIGURE 11. *Needle detail*

36

FIGURE 12. Singleleaf pinyon
SCALE: 1 x 1

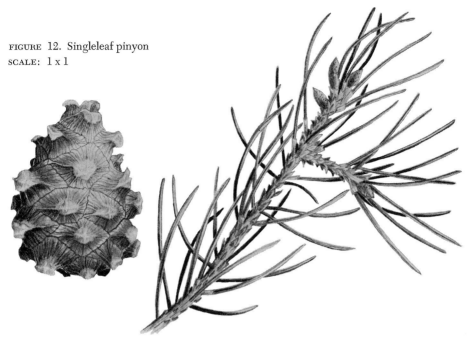

FIGURE 13. Douglas fir

FIGURE 14. Utah juniper

between the scales; buds and bud scales are sharp-pointed. Bark is gray and smooth on young trees but dark and rough on old trees.

White fir, *Abies concolor,* has needles similar to the above, about 1 to 2 inches long, flat and blunt. Its cones are erect in the top of the tree, disintegrating in place when mature in late summer or fall. Seeds are liberated at considerable distance above ground and may be easily carried by the wind. Buds are blunt and embedded in resin. This species occurs in cool shaded canyons, more abundantly at the higher altitudes. Bark on young trees is smooth and silvery, becoming black with age.

JUNIPER OR CYPRESS FAMILY, *Cupressaceae*

Native members of this family are small trees or bushy shrubs of the genus *Juniperus.* Leaves are small, scale-like and closely appressed to the twigs. Cones are berry-like with scales fleshy and fused. These trees are commonly, but erroneously, called "cedars."

14. **Utah juniper,** *Juniperus osteosperma,* is the most common species in Zion Canyon. It has rigid branchlets and "berries" about ½ inch in diameter, which are whitish at maturity.

15. **Rocky Mountain juniper,** *J. scopulorum,* is frequently seen on the plateaus and occasionally on shaded north-facing slopes of the lower side canyons. It has smaller fruits, and its branchlets are more slender and often drooping. A cultivated species of *Cupressus,* the **smooth**

FIGURE 14. *Detail of Utah juniper showing fruit*

JEROME GIFFORD

Arizona cypress, *C. glabra,* has persisted since the valley was farmed and may be seen in the old orchard at the Watchman Campground. One or two specimens of the **big tree,** *Sequoia gigantea,* of the family *Taxodiaceae,* have been planted and are thriving in the village of Springdale, near Zion National Park.

JOINT-FIR FAMILY, *Ephedraceae*

Representatives of this family are much-branched shrubs with jointed green stems. Their leaves have been reduced to very small triangular teeth which occur at each joint.

16. **Mormon tea,** *Ephedra viridis,* is a green shrub about 1 to 4 feet tall, common on the dry hot hillsides of the American Southwest up to 7,500 feet. For leaves it has 2 small triangular teeth at each joint. **Nevada ephedra,** *E. nevadensis,* is similar but somewhat coarser and of a more bluish color. It is restricted to areas below 4,500 feet. **Torrey ephedra,** *E. torreyana,* has 3 leaves at each joint. It also is bluish-green. It occurs in the Petrified Forest area of Zion. This plant was named for John Torrey, a famous botanist of the 19th century who was for many years a professor at Columbia University. He was a friend of and collaborator with Asa Gray, the well known botanist of Harvard. Dried twigs of these shrubs were used by the pioneers to make a tea. They have also been used medicinally for many years by both Indians and pioneers.

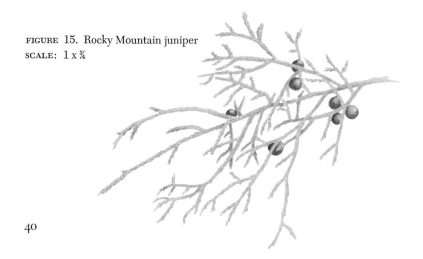

FIGURE 15. Rocky Mountain juniper
SCALE: 1 x ¾

40

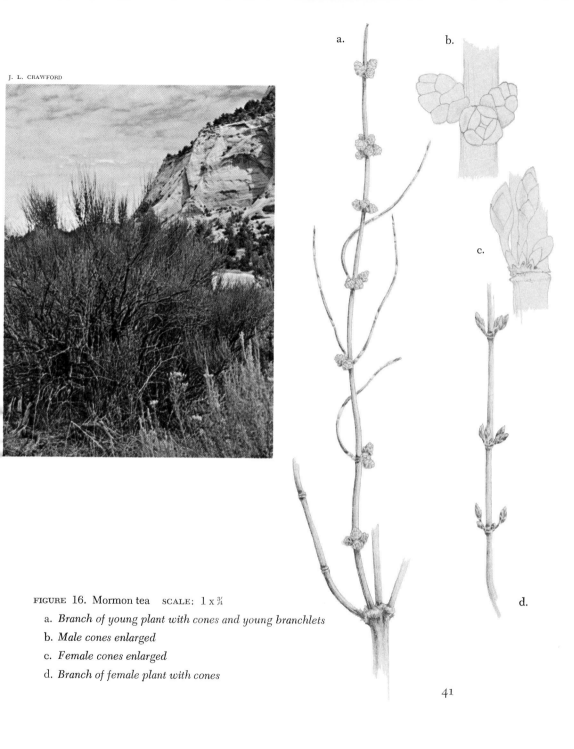

J. L. CRAWFORD

FIGURE 16. Mormon tea   SCALE: 1 x ¾

  a. *Branch of young plant with cones and young branchlets*

  b. *Male cones enlarged*

  c. *Female cones enlarged*

  d. *Branch of female plant with cones*

41

The seeds of Angiosperms are always enclosed in a receptacle formed from the ripening ovary and its coverings which becomes a seedpod or seed covering.

Key to herbs with parallel-veined leaves and with inconspicuous flowers, or at least flowers not highly colored. Flowers usually in tight or open clusters, mainly grasses or grass-like plants.

I. Plants growing on more or less dry soil.
  A. Leaves flat; stems round, hollow and jointed
                                              Grass family 43
  B. Stems round, not jointed (except sword-leaved rush, which has flat stems); flower parts in 3's or 6's   **Rush family** 54
  C. Stems usually 3-angled, triangular in cross-section
                                              Sedge family 50

II. Plants growing in water.
  A. Plants tiny, round green bodies, floating
                                          Duckweed family 52
  B. Plants standing in water but rooted in the mud of ponds or springs, or in wet sand at their margins.
    1. Plants tall, up to 6 feet. Leaves nearly 1 inch broad; flowers minute, crowded in dense brown spikes topping tall stalks   **Cattail family** 42
    2. Plants not over 3 feet tall.
      A. Stems flat; leaves nearly an inch wide
                                     Swordleaf rush 54
      B. Stems 3-cornered; leaves less than ½ inch wide
                                        Bulrush 50

CATTAIL FAMILY, *Typhaceae*

Common cattail, *Typha latifolia,* a tall plant with long flat leaves and tall stalks topped by dark brown cylindrical flower spikes, grows in marshes and shallow water.

GRASS FAMILY, *Gramineae*

This is one of the largest and most important of plant families, but because the flowers, which are wind-pollinated, are not conspicuous or brightly colored, it is not of special interest to the average observer. However grasses are of great economic importance. All of our cereal grains belong to this group which also provides much of the pasturage for livestock and game animals, besides clothing our lawns, wild meadows and hillsides. Only a few of the most easily recognized native species are described here, but a list of all those known to occur in the Park is given.

Common reed, *Phragmites australis,* is a stout grass with leafy stems which may be as much as 12 feet tall. Its inflorescence is a large plumose panicle, but in this area it seldom blooms. The stalks have been used by man for arrow shafts and weaving rods, the whole plant for thatching, and the leaves for mats, cords and nets. It grows on wet ground and is seen around springs.

Indian ricegrass, *Oryzopsis hymenoides,* is frequently seen along trails in the Park. Its inflorescence is open, and the grains, on slender stalks, are comparatively large. This plant furnishes very good forage on the sandy areas where it grows. The grains were used as food by Indians.

17. **Mutton grass,** *Poa fendleriana,* is probably the commonest spring grass in Zion Canyon and is frequent on the plateaus. It is found along all the trails, growing in clumps from 8 to 24 inches tall. Its light green oblong flower clusters are up to 5 inches long and ½ to 1 inch wide.

18. **Blue grama,** *Bouteloua gracilis,* is frequently seen on the plateaus. It is easily recognized by its dark, flag-like spikes, resembling railroad semaphore signals, 2 or 3 to each stalk held well above the usually curled leaves. **Side-oats grama,** *B. curtipendula,* with numerous short purplish spikes arranged along stalks a foot or more tall is sometimes found on dry rocky slopes of the Upper Sonoran and Transition Zones. **Sixweeks grama,** *B. barbata,* is a small annual grass with somewhat

FIGURE 17. *Seed detail*

FIGURE 17. Mutton grass
SCALE: 1 x ¾

FIGURE 18. Blue grama
SCALE: 1 x ½

prostrate stems and purple spikes about ½ inch long, found on sandy and gravelly ground below 5,000 feet. *B. uniflora* also occurs in the Park.

19. **Galleta grass,** *Hilaria jamesii*, is a dry land grass usually found in sandy areas. It has a cord-like creeping stem from which clusters of tough gray leaves and 8 to 15 inch stalks rise at intervals. The florets are grouped in clusters, and the inflorescence has a fuzzy appearance. It is a very important forage grass in arid country.

GRASS SPECIES REPORTED FOR ZION NATIONAL PARK

Agropyron cristatum	Crested wheatgrass
A. dasystachyum	Thickspike wheatgrass
A. desertorum	Desert wheatgrass
A. inerme	Smooth wheatgrass or beardless wheatgrass
A. smithii	Western wheatgrass
A. spicatum	Bluebunch wheatgrass
A. subsecundum	Bearded wheatgrass
A. trachycaulum (*A. pauciflorum*)	Slender wheatgrass
Agrostis alba	Redtop
A. scabra	Winter bentgrass
A. semiverticillata (*A. verticillata*)	Water bentgrass
Andropogon saccharoides	Silver bluestem
Aristida fendleriana	Fendler three-awn
A. glauca	Three-awn
A. longiseta	Red three-awn
Bouteloua barbata	Sixweeks grama
B. curtipendula	Side-oats grama
B. eriopoda	Black grama
B. gracilis	Blue grama
B. uniflora	One-flowered grama
Bromus anomalus	Nodding brome

46

FIGURE 19. Galleta grass
SCALE: 1 x ¾

FIGURE 19. *Flower detail*

47

B. carinatus	California brome
B. ciliatus	Fringed brome
B. inermis	Smooth brome
B. marginatus	Big mountain brome
B. polyanthus	Many-flowered brome (or mountain brome)
B. rigidus	Ripgut grass
B. rubens	Foxtail chess
B. tectorum	Cheatgrass
Cenchrus pauciflorus (C. echinatus, C. longispinus)	Sandbur
Chloris virgata	Feather fingergrass
Cynodon dactylon	Bermuda grass
Dactylis glomerata	Orchardgrass
Distichlis stricta	Desert saltgrass
Elymus canadensis	Wild rye
E. cinereus	Great Basin wild rye
Festuca microstachys	
F. octoflora	Sixweeks fescue
F. ovina	Sheep fescue
F. pacifica	Pacific fescue
Glyceria elata	Mannagrass
G. striata	Fowl mannagrass
Hilaria jamesii	Galleta
H. rigida	Big galleta
Hordeum brachyantherum (H. nodosum)	Meadow barley
H. depressum	
H. jubatum	Foxtail barley
H. stebbensii (H. murinum)	Mouse barley
Koeleria cristatum	Prairie Junegrass
Muhlenbergia andina	Foxtail muhly
M. curtifolia	
M. montana	Mountain muhly

M. porteri	Bush muhly
M. pungens	Spiny muhly
M. richardsonis	Mat muhly
M. torreyi	Ring muhly
M. wrightii	Spike muhly
Oryzopsis hymenoides	Indian ricegrass
O. bloomeri (hybrid)	Bloomer ricegrass
Panicum capillare	Witchgrass
Phleum pratense	Timothy
Phragmites australis	Common reed, canegrass
Poa bigelovii	Bigelow bluegrass
P. bulbosa	Bulbous bluegrass
P. compressa	Canada bluegrass
P. fendleriana (P. longiligula)	Muttongrass
P. nevadensis	Nevada bluegrass
P. pratensis	Kentucky bluegrass
P. sandbergii (P. secunda)	Sandberg bluegrass
P. scabrella	Pine bluegrass
Polypogon monspeliensis	Rabbitfoot grass
Puccinellia airoides	Alkaligrass
Setaria glauca (S. lutescens)	Yellow bristlegrass
Sitanion hystrix	Squirreltail
S. jubatum	Squirreltail
Sorghum halepense	Johnson grass
Sphenopholis obtusata	Prairie wedgegrass
Sporobolus contractus	Spike dropseed
S. cryptandrus	Sand dropseed
S. flexuosus	Mesa dropseed
S. giganteus	Giant dropseed
Stipa columbiana	Subalpine needlegrass
S. comata	Needle-and-thread
S. lettermanii	Letterman needlegrass
S. speciosa	Desert needlegrass
Tridens pulchella (*Triodia pulchella*)	Fluffgrass

SEDGE FAMILY, *Cyperaceae*

Sedges are grass-like plants. Most of them may be distinguished from grasses by their 3-cornered, unjointed stems. Their flowers are small and usually crowded into dense clusters. This is a very large plant family with numerous species in northern and high altitude regions, especially on wet ground. A few are known from stream banks and ponds in Zion Canyon and a few more from meadows on the plateaus.

20. **Ovalhead sedge,** *Carex festivella,* is a handsome sedge with 3-cornered stalks 1 to 3 feet tall, taller than the flat leaves. It has dark brown heads ½ to 1 inch long and grows in open woods on the plateaus.

21. **Panicled bulrush,** *Scirpus microcarpus,* is a stout leafy plant with small heads in umbellate clusters. It grows up to 4 feet tall in very wet places and may be seen in bogs along the Virgin River. **American bulrush,** S. *americanus,* which has stiff slender triangular stems from 1 to 4 feet tall, is another one of the common kinds. It occurs in swamps

FIGURE 20. Ovalhead sedge, *heads dark brown*
SCALE: 1 x ½

51

on the floor of Zion Canyon and in other wet places. Other species in this family reported for the Park are:

Carex aquatilis	Water sedge
C. aurea	Golden sedge
C. festivella	Ovalhead sedge
C. hystricina	Bottlebrush sedge
C. kelloggii	Kellogg sedge
C. microptera	Smallwing sedge
C. occidentalis	Western sedge
C. rostrata	Beaked sedge
C. vallicola	Valley sedge
Eleocharis macrostachya	Common spikerush
Scirpus acutus	Tule bulrush
S. americanus	American bulrush
S. microcarpus	Panicled bulrush
S. paludosus	Alkali bulrush
S. validus	Softstem bulrush

DUCKWEED FAMILY, *Lemnaceae*

The tiny floating green disks of these plants are the smallest seed plants known. **Common duckweed,** *Lemna minor,* occurs on the water of most of the ponds and slow-moving streams of the Park. In mid-summer and later it multiplies rapidly, forming floating masses of green which provide food for ducks. Though they are perennial flowering plants, they rarely produce seed but live over winter by sinking into the mud at the bottom of the pond. This species is widely distributed throughout the world.

SPIDERWORT FAMILY, *Commelinaceae*

22. **Spiderwort,** *Tradescantia occidentalis scopulorum,* is a plant having showy bright purplish-blue flowers with 3 petals and yellow anthers. The leaves are long and narrow; its flowers open early in the morning and soon wither. There is a sticky juice in the stem and leaves. It occurs on sandy areas throughout the Park except on the high plateaus.

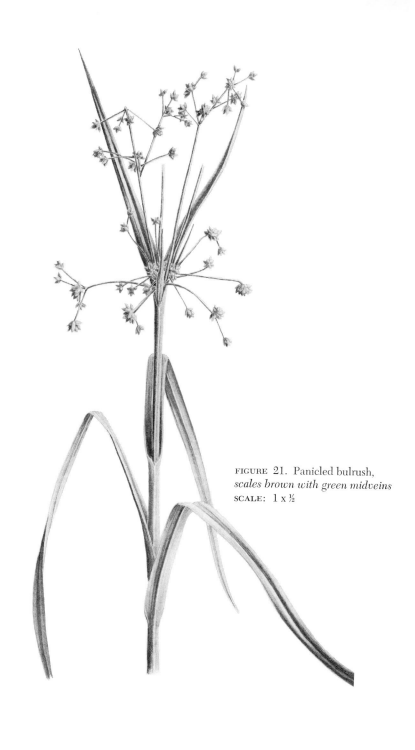

FIGURE 21. Panicled bulrush,
scales brown with green midveins
SCALE: 1 x ½

RUSH FAMILY, *Juncaceae*

This family is very closely related to the lilies. Its flowers are small and usually inconspicuous but on the same pattern as those of the lilies. There are 6 perianth segments, 6 stamens and a 3-parted stigma. Perianth segments are small and usually brown; stigmas may be pink to red and plume-like. In general these plants grow in moist areas such as meadows and along stream banks. Their stems are round and green, leaves usually inconspicuous.

Swordleaf rush, *Juncus xiphioides,* is a plant 20 to 40 inches tall with flat, iris-like leaves and an open cluster of small brownish flowers. It grows in wet sand along streams in the side canyons. Other species in this family reported for the Park are listed below:

Juncus balticus	Wiregrass
J. bufonius	Toad rush
J. mexicanus	Mexican rush
J. regellii	
J. saximontanus brunescens	
J. tenuis	
J. torreyi	Torrey rush
Luzula parviflora	Woodrush

LILY FAMILY, *Liliaceae*

The members of this family have their flower parts in 3's or 6's with 6 perianth segments (petals and sepals) which are usually colored and may be all alike or in 2 sets of 3 each. There are 6 stamens. The ovary is *superior,* and the fruit, a pod or berry, is usually 3-celled, sometimes appearing 6-celled because of a partial division of each cell. The leaves are parallel-veined.

I. Stalks leafy.

23. **Fritillary,** *Fritillaria atropurpurea,* is 10 to 18 inches tall with brownish or purplish flowers with purple spots. The leaves are well scattered on the stems. It grows in sandy woods.

54

FIGURE 22. Spiderwort

FIGURE 23. Fritillary,
flowers with brownish or purple spots

24. **Fairybells,** *Disporum trachycarpum,* is a rare plant of cool canyons, usually above 5,500 feet, with a stout stem and broad oval leaves; its flowers are inconspicuous, but the fruit is a red 3-lobed berry.

25. **Star-flowered solomon plume,** *Smilacina stellata,* has white star-like flowers less than ½ inch broad, in a short raceme at the end of a leafy stem. It is common on many shaded slopes, especially at Weeping Rock and in the Narrows. A stouter species with smaller but more densely clustered flowers is *Smilacina racemosa.* It occurs in similar locations. These plants spread by underground stems.

II. Stalks without leaves; leaves in a basal cluster.

    A. Leaves stiff, very sharp-pointed, a foot or more long.   **Yucca**

FIGURE 24. Fairy bells

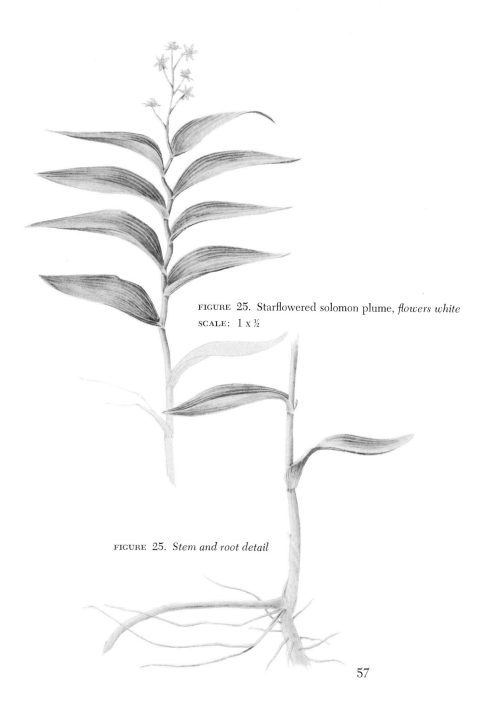

FIGURE 25. Starflowered solomon plume, *flowers white*
SCALE: 1 x ½

FIGURE 25. *Stem and root detail*

57

26. **Spanish bayonet** or **narrowleaf yucca,** *Yucca angustissima,* is a large stout plant with very sharp-pointed leaves. Its flower stalk may be 6 feet or more in height. The individual flowers are creamy white, 6-petaled and occur in a large open cluster along the upper part of the stalk. The seedpods are dry and woody. Another species occurring in the Park is 27. **Datil yucca,** *Y. baccata,* with wider grayish-green leaves and a shorter flower stalk. The datil seedpods are fleshy and have been used for food. A good place to see both kinds of yucca is in the planters in front of the Visitor Center.

      B. Leaves not stiff nor very sharp.

           1. Flowers in clusters (umbels) at top of stalk, perianth segments 6.

                A. Flowers blue or purplish   28. **Bluedicks Funnellily**

FIGURE 26. Spanish bayonet

FIGURE 26. *Detail*

ALLEN MALMQUIST

ALLEN MALMQUIST

FIGURE 27. Datil yucca

28. **Bluedicks,** *Brodiaea pulchella pauciflora,* is found in many parts of the Park. The funnel-shaped blue flowers are clustered at the tip of a long, often bending stalk. The leaves are very long and narrow and occur only at the base of the stalk. **Funnellily,** *Androstephium breviflorum,* is similar, but its stem is usually stouter and shorter and its flowers are paler. Each perianth segment has a dark stripe.

B. Flowers pink or white   **Wild onion**

Wild onion, *Allium,* may be easily recognized by the onion odor of the leaves.

29. **Nevada wild onion,** A. *nevadense cristatum,* has a pale pink or white perianth with the segments marked by a dark line. Each plant has one leaf, longer than the flower stalk and often coiled at the tip. This plant grows in stony soil and has been found near the Petrified Forest.

FIGURE 28.
Flower, side view

FIGURE 28. Bluedicks,
stem smooth, leafless
SCALE: 1 x ½

60

FIGURE 29. Nevada wild onion

SCALE: 1 x 1

30. **Tapertip onion,** A. *acuminatum,* has its bright pink flowers in an umbel. Its petals are drawn out into long slender points. A. *palmeri,* which also occurs in the Park, is similar.

     2. Flowers in an elongated, terminal cluster or arranged along the stem, cream-colored   **Death camas**

Two species of **Death camas,** *Zigadenus,* are found in the Park.

31. **Foothill death camas,** Z. *paniculatus,* occurs at lower altitudes and sometimes also on the plateaus. Its cream-colored flowers are small. A more handsome kind is Z. *elegans,* also cream-colored and with a yellow splotch at the base of each segment of the perianth. This plant is usually found at the higher altitudes. Its flowers appear as 6-pointed stars scattered along the stem. Both these species are poisonous, and care should be taken that they are not tasted.

     3. Flowers single or few, petals 3, 1 to 2 inches long

Mariposa lily

Some of the most beautiful flowers of this family are the **Mariposa lilies,** species of *Calochortus.*

FIGURE 30. Tapertip onion

FIGURE 31. Foothill death camas

FIGURE 33. Bentstem mariposa

32. **Sego lily,** *C. nuttallii,* is the state flower of Utah. The 3 ivory-white, or sometimes lavender, petals each have a dark splotch at their base. There is also a yellow variety. The bulbs of the sego lilies were an important food for Mormon pioneers when they arrived in Utah Territory. Thomas Nuttall, for whom this plant was named, was an English-American naturalist of the early nineteenth century. He travelled widely in what is now the western United States, collecting and studying birds and plants and describing many new species of both.

33. **Bentstem mariposa,** *C. flexuosus,* with pinkish-lavender blossoms, has a flexible stem, as its Latin name implies, and tends to lean on nearby plants. It is often found on the dry brushy areas of the Upper and Lower Sonoran Zones.

FIGURE 32. Sego lily

ALLEN MALMQUIST

64

ALLEN MALMQUIST

IRIS FAMILY, *Iridaceae*

Plants of this group have long, narrow leaves and flower parts in 3's. They differ from the lilies in having the corolla and stamens located on top of the ovary, that is, the ovary is in an *inferior* position. The only local representative of the family is one species of **blue-eyed grass,** *Sisyrinchium demissum,* which is rare in the Park. It has grass-like leaves, and its blue flowers open only in bright sunlight.

ORCHID FAMILY, *Orchidaceae*

These flowers have 6 segments united into an irregular perianth which usually has one segment modified into a sac-like lip and one which may have a spur. The pistil and stamens are united. Fertilization is by insects especially adapted to this particular flower structure.

34. **Giant helleborine,** *Epipactis gigantea,* is the most frequently seen species. Its stem may be from 8 to about 40 inches long, but locally is usually a foot or less. Ovate or longer leaves are scattered along it with a few greenish or purplish flowers, each having a sac-like lip. It grows in rock crevices in many seepage areas or on wet ground.

Rattlesnake plantain, *Goodyera oblongifolia,* with dark green basal leaves mottled with white, has a 6 to 8 inch stalk which bears a raceme of small, greenish-white flowers. It is found in cool, moist, shaded situations as in Hidden Canyon. **Few-flowered bog orchid,** or **canyon bog orchid,** *Habenaria sparsiflora,* with yellowish-green flowers along the upper stem, occurs in moist, shaded places on the plateaus. **White bog orchid,** *H. dilatata,* has been reported.

FIGURE 34. Giant helleborine,
flowers greenish or purplish
SCALE: 1 x 1¼

Key to many of the common woody plants (trees or shrubs) with broad, at least not needle-like, leaves.

I. Leaves evergreen.
    A. Leaves opposite.
        1. Leaves dull and leathery, 2 to 3 inches long
                                      133. **Silk-tassel** 190
        2. Leaves smooth, shiny, ½ to 1 inch long
                              113. **Myrtle pachystima** 166
    B. Leaves alternate.
        1. Bark smooth and reddish   135. **Manzanita** 194
        2. Bark gray, more or less rough; leaves with sharp-pointed teeth.
            A. Leaves compound, stems trailing
                          67. **Creeping hollygrape** 110
            B. Leaves simple, stems erect   38. **Shrub live oak** 74
II. Leaves very tiny, resembling juniper leaves; plumy-branched shrubs found along stream beds   fig. VII. **Tamerisk** 170
III. Leaves pinnately compound, not evergreen.
    A. Leaves and branches oppositely arranged.
        1. Trees, below 5,000 feet.
            A. Leaflets with smooth edges   137. **Velvet ash** 196

68

2. Leaves alternate, sometimes clustered.

    A. Leaves very narrow, sticky above, white beneath

                                                     Yerbasanta 208

    B. Leaves narrow, smooth, 3-veined; flowers composite in small heads arranged in loose clusters

                                                  178. Emory baccharis 252

    C. Leaves silvery gray, narrow; at lowest altitudes

                                                  Arrowweed 252

    D. Leaves smooth, clustered, widening and rounded at outer end   **Squawapple** 136

    E. Leaves round, toothed around outer end; flowers white, in clusters   90, 91. **Serviceberry** 134

    F. Leaves uneven at base, strongly veined beneath

                                        39. **Hackberry** 76

C. Seeds long-tailed; leaves may be evergreen.

  1. Leaves about ½ inch long, 3 or 5-lobed, white beneath; flowers pale yellow or whitish   87. **Cliffrose** 132

  2. Leaves very narrow, evergreen, margins inrolled; often grows in crevices of slickrock

                          94. **Littleleaf mountain mahogany** 140

  3. Leaves wedge-shaped at base, more or less toothed

                      Alderleaf mountain mahogany 140

This family includes the willows and cottonwoods (poplars), which are deciduous trees or shrubs with alternate leaves and flowers in catkins. Male and female flowers are on different plants. The catkins often, but not always, appear before the leaves. The ripe catkins are made up of many small pods, and those of cottonwood trees appear like a string of beads. The little pods each contain many tiny seeds. When they split, the seeds are liberated and float away, each carried on the wind by a tuft of white hairs. This is the "cotton" characteristic of these trees.

Cottonwood or **poplar,** *Populus.* The most common tree on the floor of the canyon and along the larger streams is the **Fremont cottonwood,** *P. fremontii.* When mature the trees are large and widely branched. Old trees take on a gnarled, picturesque appearance. Cottonwood leaves are firm in texture and turn to brilliant gold in late autumn. A second species, the **narrowleaf cottonwood,** *P. angustifolia,* is rare in the Park, known to occur only in the upper part of the Narrows.

Quaking aspen, *P. tremuloides,* occurs at the highest altitudes, consequently is seldom seen by Park visitors. It is a small, white-barked tree with roundish leaves on slender petioles which are flattened oppositely to the leaf blades. This results in the noticeable and almost constant trembling of the leaves. In autumn the trees become golden.

Willow, *Salix.* Willows may be distinguished from all other trees or shrubs by their single bud scale which appears like a cap over the bud. A few species of willow form small trees up to about 30 feet in height. The most handsome of these is the **red willow** or **polished willow,** *S. laevigata.* It occurs on the main canyon floor and in some side canyons such as Heaps Canyon. Leaves are dark green and shiny above, white beneath. They are lanceolate in shape with a long tapering tip. The **arroyo willow,** *S. lasiolepis,* also has leaves which are white beneath, but not so shiny above. These leaves are obovate and the tip varies from rounded to sharp-pointed. **Whiplash willow,** *S. lasiandra caudata,* has leaves which are green on both sides but somewhat shiny and a little lighter beneath. They are obovate in shape and abruptly sharp-

71

pointed. Several other species of willow which usually grow from 6 to 12 feet tall are more often seen at higher altitudes.

The shrub willows are difficult to distinguish. 35. **Sandbar** or **coyote willow,** S. *exigua,* is the most common species. It is about 5 to 15 feet tall and has narrow grayish leaves. It occurs abundantly along streams, especially on moist, sandy areas, forming dense thickets, especially along the Virgin River in Zion Canyon. The following kinds occur in the Park:

Salix drummondiana	Drummond willow
S. geyeriana	Geyer willow
S. lutea (S. watsonii)	Yellow willow
S. myrtilifolia (S. pseudocordata)	Blueberry willow
S. nigra venulosa	Black willow
S. scouleriana	Scouler willow

BIRCH FAMILY, *Betulaceae*

36. **Water** or **river birch,** *Betula occidentalis (B. fontinalis),* is the only local species in the family. It occurs along streams or in wet areas

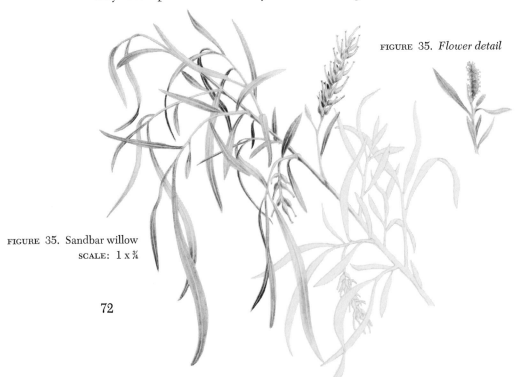

FIGURE 35. *Flower detail*

FIGURE 35. Sandbar willow
SCALE: 1 x ¾

FIGURE 36. Water birch, *bark glossy brown*
SCALE: 1 x ¾

throughout the western United States. It is usually a large shrub with several stems, delicate in aspect. Its shining dark reddish-brown bark and dainty leaves make it easy to recognize. Before the leaves appear in spring, it puts out long staminate catkins which hang from the twigs, shedding quantities of yellow pollen. The pistillate catkins are shorter and brown. After fertilization these develop into papery cone-like structures which contain the seeds. This birch is found along streams and near springs in Zion's side canyons.

OAK FAMILY, *Fagaceae*

There are three species of oak in Zion. 37. **Gambel oak,** *Quercus gambelii,* is the commonest and largest in the main canyon. It sometimes forms low spreading trees; more often it occurs in shrubby thickets. Its deciduous leaves are firm and slightly rough with rounded lobes. It occurs throughout the Park.

38. **Shrub live oak,** *Q. turbinella,* forms low thickets and has grayish-green prickle-lobed holly-like leaves. It is abundant on the dry slopes around the canyon and on the plateaus. It retains its leaves through the winter. The **wavyleaf oak,** *Q. undulata,* is a similar species with less sharply toothed leaves which drop off in winter.

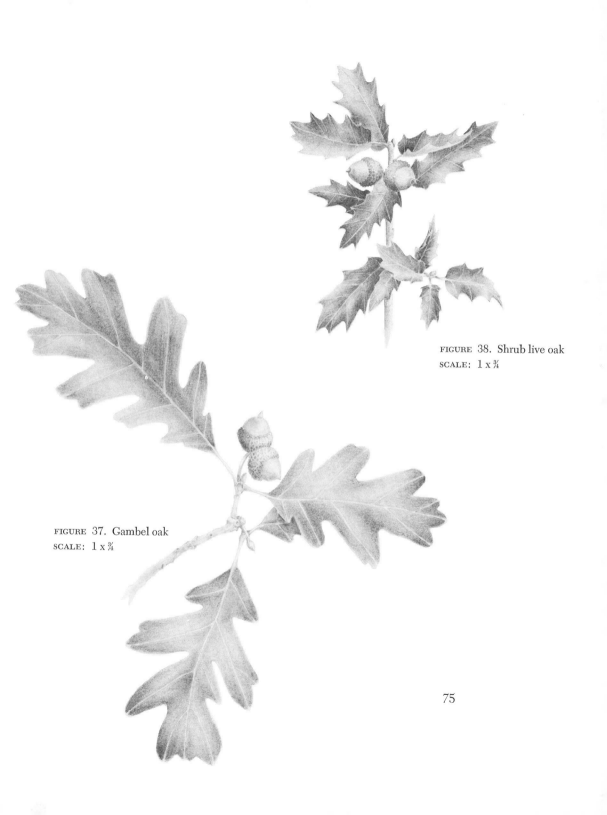

FIGURE 38. Shrub live oak
SCALE: 1 x ¾

FIGURE 37. Gambel oak
SCALE: 1 x ¾

75

ELM FAMILY, *Ulmaceae*

39. **Hackberry,** *Celtis reticulata,* is a small tree or shrub common on the floor and lower slopes of the canyon. The base of the leaf is uneven. These trees present a beautifully lacy appearance in spring when the young leaves first appear with the many small green flowers. The fruit is a small sweet berry. This tree is very susceptible to insect and fungus infestation, and most individuals are deformed by numerous galls and witches'-brooms. Leaves are often ragged and perforated by chewing insects.

MULBERRY FAMILY, *Moraceae*

American hop, *Humulus americanus,* is a green-stemmed, twining vine with opposite, deeply 3 to 7 palmately lobed leaves and drooping, papery bracted seed clusters. It occurs along the Narrows Trail and at Weeping Rock.

NETTLE FAMILY, *Urticaceae*

This family is represented by one inconspicuous species, **pellitory,** *Parietaria obtusa,* which is unnettle-like in that it has no stinging hairs. It occurs in Coalpits Wash.

MISTLETOE FAMILY, *Loranthaceae*

This is a group of plants parasitic on members of the pine and cypress families. Their seedlings produce root-like structures which anchor the plant and are able to penetrate the bark of the host tree. These little strands grow through the living tissue of the inner bark, from which they draw nourishment and eventually sap the vitality of the host. This makes the infected trees more susceptible to other parasites.

76

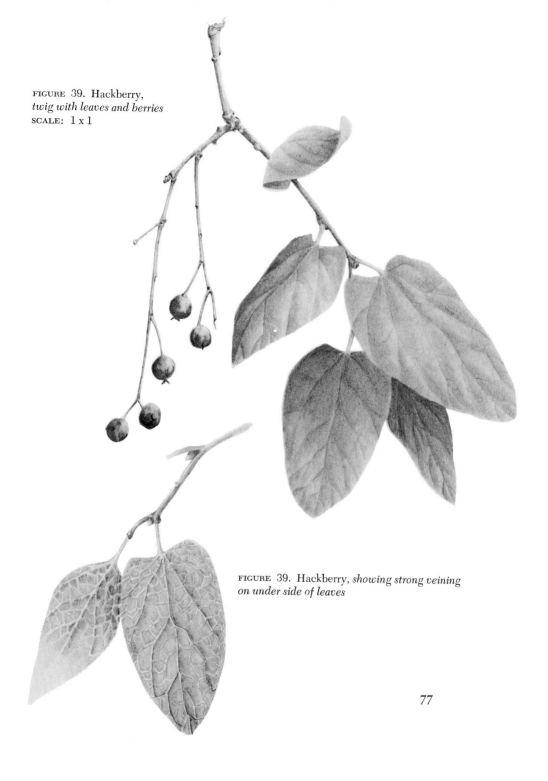

FIGURE 39. Hackberry,
twig with leaves and berries
SCALE: 1 x 1

FIGURE 39. Hackberry, *showing strong veining
on under side of leaves*

77

40. **Juniper mistletoe,** *Phoradendron juniperinum,* is frequently seen as clusters of jointed, yellowish-green stems sprouting from branches of the Utah juniper. Its small, scale-like leaves are oppositely arranged. It produces numerous small clusters of pearl-like berries containing very sticky seeds. Birds feed on these and so distribute the parasite. Three other species of a different genus, *Arceuthobium,* occur in the Park: *A. campylopodum* on both kinds of pinyon; *A. douglasii* on white fir and Douglas fir; *A. vaginatum* on ponderosa pine.

SANDALWOOD FAMILY, *Santalaceae*

This family is represented by only one species, 41. **comandra,** *Comandra pallida,* a plant 6 to 10 inches high with pale green leaves and small greenish-white flowers. It grows in many sandy areas of the Sonoran Zones.

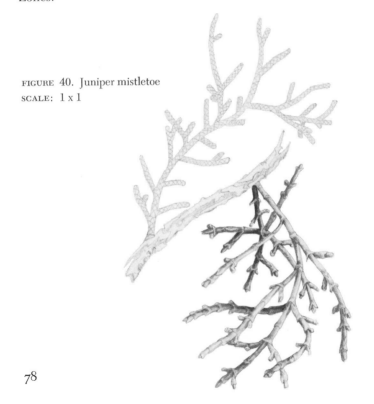

FIGURE 40. Juniper mistletoe
SCALE: 1 x 1

FIGURE 41. Comandra

BUCKWHEAT FAMILY, *Polygonaceae*

This is a large family which includes many differing species. Its individual flowers are very small, mostly yellow or pinkish-white. Some kinds have so many flowers, often crowded together, that the plants are quite conspicuous. There are no petals, only small petal-like sepals which are joined and collectively called a *perianth*. The most noticeable kinds have their flowers in *umbels*, i.e. umbrella-like arrangements (ill. p. 317). Other kinds have papery sheaths surrounding the stem at its joints. The "seeds" are often 3-sided and shiny black. Botanically these are 1-seeded fruits, properly called *achenes*. The genus *Eriogonum* is represented by many species in this area.

Eriogonum (pronounced Er i og' o num), *Eriogonum*. This group may be divided into those with umbrella-like flower clusters and those with flowers in other sorts of arrangements. Some are repeatedly 2-forked. Eriogonum has white, pinkish, or yellow flowers which change color as they age so that often the color of the flower clusters will be mixed. The white ones turn pinkish or even red and the yellow ones turn reddish or rust color. Often the leaves are cottony white, at least beneath, and frequently the leaf margins are inrolled. Most of the species flower in late summer or fall.

I. Flowers in definite umbels; perennial plants.

42. **Sulphur flower**, *E. umbellatum*, is a variable species. Ordinarily the flowers are a bright yellow, becoming rusty when they begin to age. Some forms are pale or cream-colored. Leaves taper to a slender stalk at the base and are mostly pointed at the tip; leaves and stalks may be more or less covered with cottony hairs. These plants are somewhat woody at the base. The local variety is *E. umbellatum subaridum*, which has compact, round, bright yellow umbels. It often grows up through shrubs and occurs on the East Zion Plateau and in other places.

43. **Slickrock sulphur flower**, *E. jamesii rupicola* (*E. flavum*), is similar but much smaller. It grows from sandstone crevices where it forms mats of short-stalked leaves ½ inch or less in length which are white beneath. Its stalks are only a few inches tall, bearing one or few umbels of bright yellow flowers. *E. corymbosum* is a much-branched plant with

8o

FIGURE 42. Sulphur flowe

ALLEN MALMQUIST

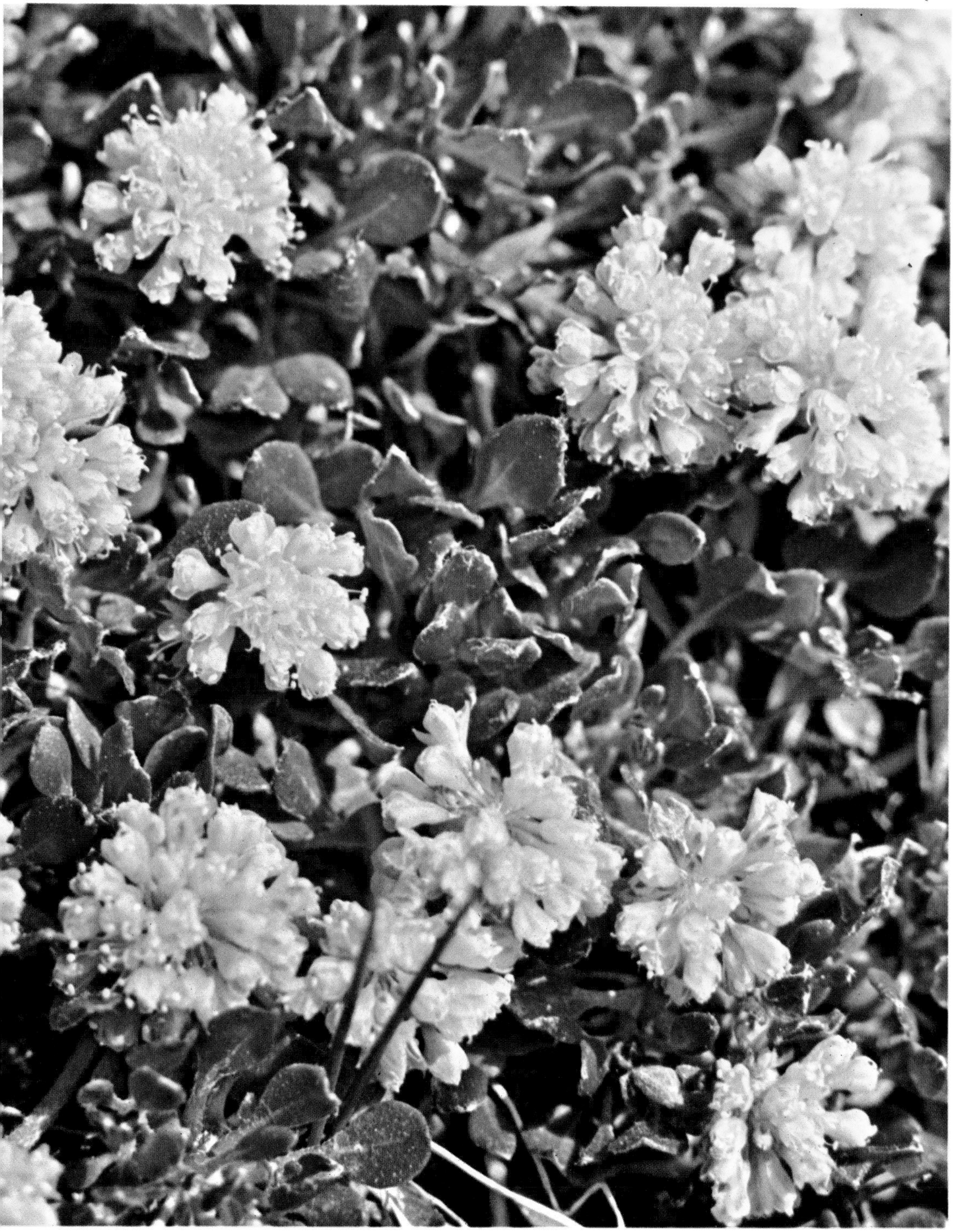

either white or yellow flowers. **Thompson eriogonum,** *E. thompsonae,* is a much-branched plant up to a foot tall with yellow flowers. Leaves are long-stalked and white beneath. It forms low clumps on rocky slopes in the lower part of the main canyon and along the Watchman Trail.

44. **White-flowered thompson eriogonum,** *E. thompsonae albiflorum,* is a similar but white-flowered variety which often occurs with the yellow form. The yellow one was originally collected by Mrs. Ellen Thompson, sister of Major John Wesley Powell, during the time the Powell party was at Kanab, Utah, preparing for the 1871 expedition down the Colorado River. The specimen, with others from the area, was sent to the Gray Herbarium at Harvard, where the botanist, Dr. Sereno Watson, named it for the collector.

II. Flowers variously arranged, stalks tall and mostly leafless; plants perennial.

SCALE: 1 x 1½

FIGURE 43.
Slickrock sulphur flower
(Picture taken in November)

ROBERT FOSTER

82

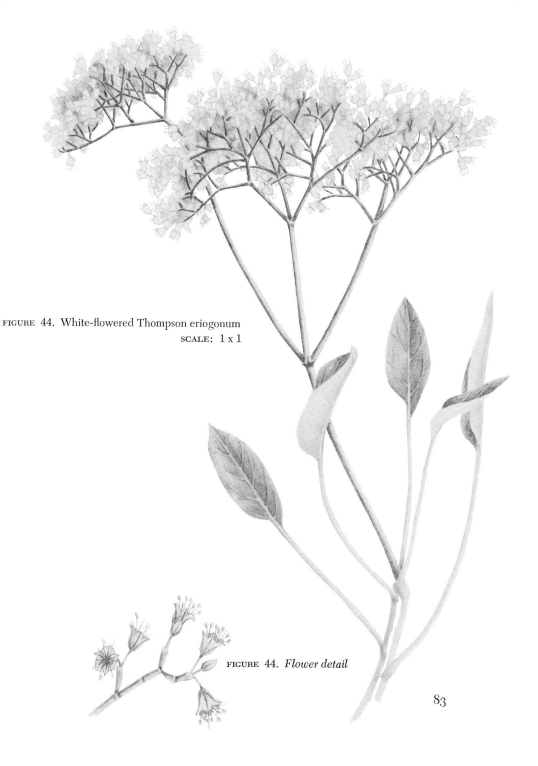

FIGURE 44. White-flowered Thompson eriogonum

SCALE: 1 x 1

FIGURE 44. *Flower detail*

83

45. **Zion desert trumpet,** *E. zionis,* has grayish stalks which are somewhat inflated. Flowers are white or pinkish, with narrow green stripes, and occur in small clusters along the upper branches. Leaves are basal, heart-shaped or ovate, white underneath. This species is an *endemic,* thought to occur only in Zion National Park.

46. **Desert trumpet,** *E. inflatum,* has stems from 1 to 2 feet tall with inflated sections. The yellow flowers are very tiny and borne on thread-like stalks. The ovate or heart-shaped green leaves on long stalks are all basal. Another tall species is the **winged eriogonum,** *E. alatum.* Its long narrow leaves are all basal. The flower cluster is branched and open with small yellowish flowers. The achenes (seeds) are about ¼ inch long and conspicuously 3-winged. This is most often seen at the higher altitudes of the Park among ponderosa pines. **Redroot eriogonum,** *E. racemosum,* is another tall slender species having 2 or 3 erect branches lined with small clusters of pinkish flowers. The leaves are basal, oval to roundish, on stalks as long as the blades, and are white beneath. It also occurs in the pine forests, as does *E. panguicense.*

III. Annual species, widely branched with white to pinkish flowers.

FIGURE 45. Zion desert trumpet, *stems are inflated*
SCALE: 1 x ¼

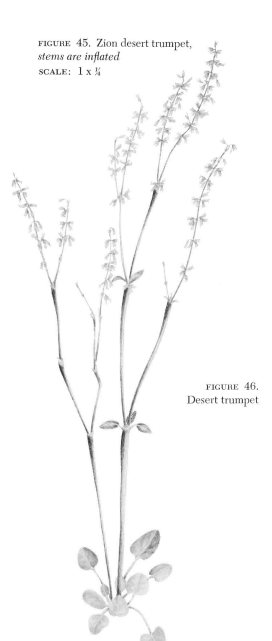

FIGURE 46. Desert trumpet

47. **Nodding eriogonum,** *E. cernuum,* is from 4 to 20 inches tall and much-branched. The white or pinkish flowers hang down from short stalks bent downwards or extending at right angles to the branches. Basal leaves are roundish and white beneath. A similar species is *E. subreniforme.* Its flowers, on thread-like stalks, are less definitely nodding. Another kind, less widely branched and with grayish stems, is the **broom eriogonum,** *E. davidsonii.* **Sorrel eriogonum,** *E. polycladon,* with pink flowers and tall gray stems occurs on roadsides and washes.

IV. Woody species, small shrubs; flowers mostly white or pinkish.

48. **California buckwheat,** *E. fasciculatum,* is a small much-branched bush. Flowers are in tight round clusters at the tips of leafless stalks which rise from leafy branches. Leaves are narrow with inrolled edges

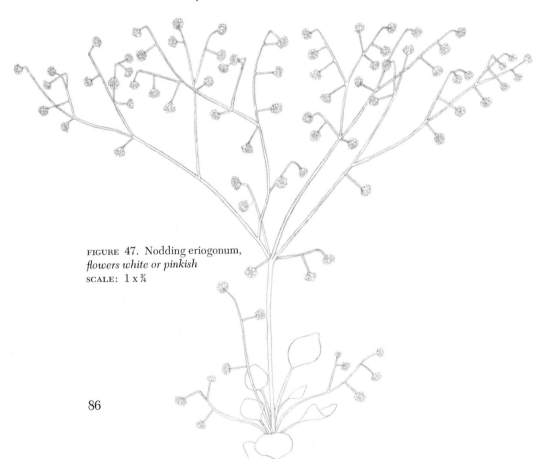

FIGURE 47. Nodding eriogonum, *flowers white or pinkish*
SCALE: 1 x ¾

86

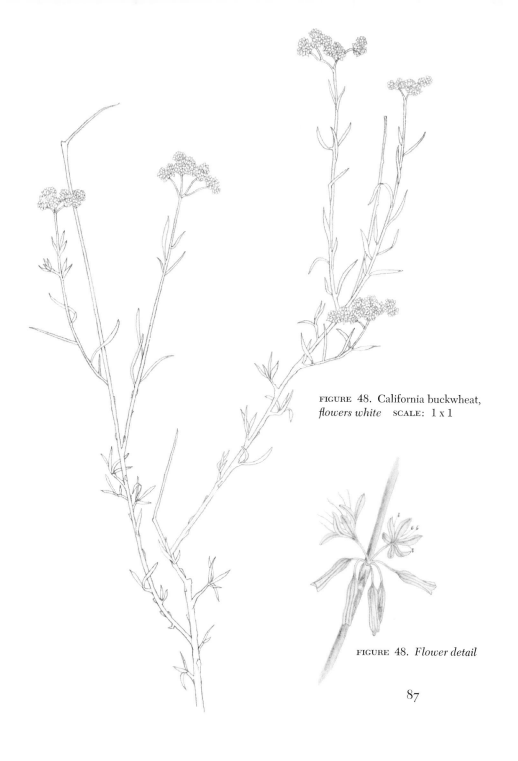

FIGURE 48. California buckwheat,
flowers white SCALE: 1 x 1

FIGURE 48. *Flower detail*

87

and are usually more or less clustered. It occurs on dry rocky slopes and is an excellent source of nectar, from which bees make honey.

Slenderbush eriogonum, *E. microthecum,* is a bushy plant about 1 foot tall with narrow leaves which have inrolled margins. Flower clusters are more open than in the above. It is commonly found on dry rocky slopes of the side canyons.

Knotweed, *Polygonum.* These are usually inconspicuous plants; many of them called "weeds."

49. **Sawatch knotweed,** *P. sawatchense,* is an interesting one. It is a low-branched annual plant with ascending branches lined with small white or pinkish flowers. Each sepal has a green stripe. The 3-cornered achenes are black and shiny. This plant grows in sandy areas and is especially noticeable after rainy periods, particularly on the East Zion Plateau. **Douglas knotweed,** *P. douglasii,* is similar. It has fewer, more erect branches and longer leaves. **Bushy knotweed,** *P. ramosissimum,* is sometimes found. It is usually much-branched and yellowish-green in color. The achenes are black but not shiny. **Prostrate knotweed,** *P. aviculare,* is sometimes found around buildings or on disturbed ground. It is a low spreading plant with its branches pressed to the earth. **Cornbind,** *P. convolvulus,* is a twining plant of roadsides or cultivated ground with arrowhead-shaped leaves.

Thurber chorizanthe (pronounced kor i zan' the), *Chorizanthe thurberi,* is an interesting rare little annual. The tiny flowers are surrounded by spine-tipped bracts which give it a starry appearance. The whole plant may be more or less reddish. The stems are repeatedly 2-forked. The small leaves, which widen towards the outer end, are all at the base.

FIGURE 49. Sawatch knotweed
SCALE: 1 x 1

Dock, *Rumex,* these are large coarse plants with big leaves and tall large clusters of small green flowers which ripen to achenes, each surrounded by reddish or rust-colored sepals. The garden rhubarb is a member of this group.

50. **Canaigre** or **wild rhubarb,** *R. hymenosepalus,* is a handsome plant with its tall fruiting panicles. Each flower has 6 sepals. Three of these become enlarged, membranous and rose or red in color when in fruit. The stalks of the leaves were used as rhubarb by Indians and Mexicans. **Curly dock,** *R. crispus,* **Mexican dock,** *R. mexicanus,* and **Utah dock,** *R. utahensis,* also occur in the Park. The first two are common plants in the Rocky Mountain region.

GOOSEFOOT FAMILY, *Chenopodiaceae*

This is another family in which there are many weedy species, and also vegetables such as beets and spinach. Flowers of all are inconspicuous, but the fruits are sometimes noticeable.

Saltbush or **shadscale,** *Atriplex.* Some members of this genus are shrubs, abundant in desert areas, especially where the soil is alkaline.

51. **Four-wing saltbush,** *A. canescens,* is a shrub found on lower canyon slopes and where the canyons open into the valley. Its leaves are gray, and it usually displays clusters of papery fruits, each one having 4 wings. Closely related to this is the **shadscale,** *A. confertifolia.* It is similar in appearance but its branchlets often become spiny. These plants are important to wildlife. They are much browsed by deer. Indians used the seeds to make meal.

FIGURE 50. Canaigre

FIGURE 51. Fourwing saltbush
SCALE: 1 x 1

91

Goosefoot or **pigweed,** *Chenopodium.* **Lambsquarters,** *C. album,* is a common plant around buildings and one that is often cooked as a pot-herb. **Fremont goosefoot,** *C. fremontii,* and *C. leptophyllum* occur in the Park. **Russian thistle,** *Salsola kali,* which is not a true thistle but does have many short spines, is a much-branched plant up to 2 or 3 feet tall which occurs on disturbed soil and forms "tumbleweeds." This plant is not a native American but was introduced from Europe and has become widely distributed along roadsides and on plains in the United States.

AMARANTH FAMILY, *Amaranthaceae*

Pigweed, *Amaranthus graecizans,* has been found near the East Entrance. It is a native. *A. alba* is a native of tropical America which occurs on disturbed soil near the Visitor Center.

FOUR-O'CLOCK FAMILY, *Nyctaginaceae*

52. **Colorado four-o'clock,** *Mirabilis multiflora,* is a plant with dark green, rounded or heart-shaped leaves, growing in low mounds on roadsides or among rocks. It is covered with brilliant purple, funnel-shaped flowers in early summer and often again after the late summer rains. These resemble the garden four-o'clocks and, like them, open late in the day and wither in bright morning sunshine. **Trailing allionia,** *Allionia incarnata (Wedeliella incarnata),* is a low spreading sticky plant with small pink flowers, found in Coalpits Wash.

FIGURE 52. Colorado four-o'clock

53. **Fragrant sand-verbena,** *Abronia fragrans*, has clusters of flowers at the ends of leafless stalks. Each cluster is surrounded by an involucre of papery bracts. Each individual flower consists of a slender tube about 1 inch long which flares out into what the botanists call a "limb" which has ruffled edges (see drawing). The species here are low spreading plants, hairy and sticky, and have white or cream-colored flowers. The showy, well-known, low desert sand-verbena blossoms are bright pink and not found in Zion. The following additional species occur in Zion National Park: *A. pumila* and *A. salsa. A. salsa* is much more sticky than the others and is usually found covered with sand particles. These plants grow in sandy or rocky places.

FIGURE 53. Fragrant sand-verbena

FIGURE 53. *Upper portion of fragrant sand-verbena*
SCALE: 1 x 1

FIGURE 53. *Basal leaves and lower stem*

The plants of this family are more or less succulent, and some of them have furnished food for Indians and pioneers. They usually have 4 or 5 very delicate petals and 2 sepals, except in *Lewisia,* which has more of both.

54. **Lanceleaf spring beauty,** *Claytonia lanceolata,* is a common plant on moist banks in spring, and in cool canyons in early summer. Each stem has a pair of narrow leaves and a stalk bearing several dainty blooms. The fragile white petals have pink veins.

55. **Southwestern lewisia** or **bitterroot,** *Lewisia brachycalyx,* a spring flower of the high plateaus, is a low plant consisting of a cluster of fleshy leaves at ground level surrounding delicate white flowers 1 or 2

FIGURE 54. Lanceleaf spring beauty,
petals veined with pink
SCALE: 1 x 1

FIGURE 55. Southwestern lewisia

97

inches across. There are several petals; the leaves taper to a stalk which has thin, transparent edges, and all grow from a thick, starchy root. The genus *Lewisia* was named for the explorer, Meriwether Lewis, who, with William Clark, led an expedition to the Oregon coast in 1804–1806. At one time when their food supply was very low, they were introduced by their Indian guide to the starch-filled roots of the northwestern bitterroot, a close relative of the local plant, which they found abundant and nutritious.

56. **Miners** or **Indian lettuce,** *Montia perfoliata,* is abundant on moist, shaded banks, as below Weeping Rock and other similar locations. The two upper leaves are joined into a saucer or cup-shaped collar below the flower stalk. There are several small flowers in a somewhat one-sided arrangement. There are at least three varieties in the Park which are difficult to distinguish: *M. perfoliata parviflora, M. perfoliata depressa,* and *M. perfoliata utahensis.* The latter seems more compact than the others. **Common purslane,** *Portulaca oleracea,* a low growing plant, naturalized from Europe, with thick leaves and pale yellow flowers, has been found on disturbed soil near the Visitor Center. **Prairie fameflower,** *Talinum parviflorum,* is a small succulent plant with a tuft of tapering cylindrical leaves at the top of a thick root. It has open clusters of small 4 or 5-petaled pink or whitish flowers. This plant seems quite rare in Zion but has been found on the sandstone ledges of the East Zion Plateau.

SCALE: 1 x 1

FIGURE 56. Miners lettuce
SCALE: 1 x 2

99

This is a group characterized by opposite leaves placed at the enlarged joints of the stem and by 5 petals. The carnation and garden pinks belong to this family.

57. **Shrubby sandwort,** *Arenaria macradenia,* is a plant with very narrow, sharp-pointed, stiff leaves and 5-petaled white flowers. Its stems are about a foot tall. It often grows from crevices in rocks and has a rather woody base. **Eastwood sandwort,** A. *eastwoodiae adenophora,* is somewhat similar. It is a more compact plant with its leaves mostly clustered at the base. Its stems are 6 to 10 inches tall, the flowers less conspicuous than in the former, with reddish petals which are shorter than the sepals. It is not as common as the first but grows in similar places. A different sandwort is *A. lanuginosa (A. confusa).* This is a plant with soft leaves and weak stems which grows in moist places under overhanging rocks, as at the Narrows. A tiny slender plant, 1 to 3 inches tall, is *A. pusilla,* which has been found on moist soil on the East Rim near Cable Mountain.

58. **James starwort** or **tuber starwort,** *Stellaria jamesiana,* usually grows in the shade of shrubs on the high plateaus. Its opposite leaves taper to a long point but are not stiff. The white flowers may be from 1 to 1½ inches across, with petals twice as long as the sepals. It has tubers on its roots. **Longleaf starwort,** S. *longifolia,* is a small delicate plant with 4-angled stems found in moist, shaded places. Its opposite leaves are narrow and pointed, 1 to 3 inches long. It has small white flowers with the petals shorter than the pointed green sepals. Other plants in this family which have been reported for the Park are **Drummond cockle,** *Lychnis drummondii,* **Scouler silene,** *Silene scouleri,* and *S. antirrhina.*

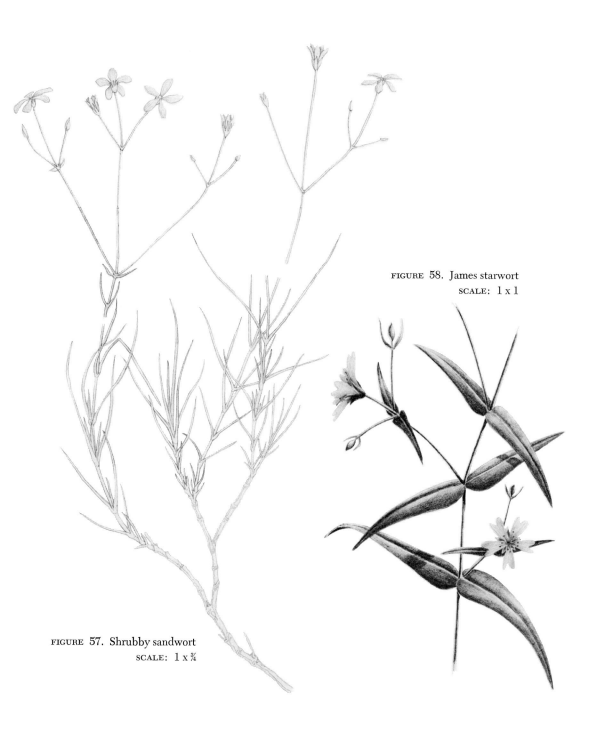

FIGURE 58. James starwort
SCALE: 1 x 1

FIGURE 57. Shrubby sandwort
SCALE: 1 x ¾

BUTTERCUP or CROWFOOT FAMILY, *Ranunculaceae*

The members of this large family show a great variety of form. An amateur can only learn to recognize the group by experience, but the characters given in the following key may help to identify some kinds.

I. Plants climbing by twining leafstalks; stems more or less woody; leaves compound; fruits are fluffy clusters of long-tailed achenes. There are no petals, but the sepals are petal-like   **Clematis**

Virginsbower, *Clematis ligusticifolia,* has clustered white flowers. It clambers over shrubs in ravines, along streams and at the edge of meadows and is conspicuous in fall because of the white fluffy fruits.

59. **Subalpine clematis,** *C. pseudoalpina,* has blue flowers, each with 4 long-pointed sepals and numerous white stamens and pistils at the center. The fruit consists of clusters of long-tailed achenes. This plant of moist woods grows at high altitudes in the Park.

II. Plants with erect or, in *Ranunculus cymbalaria,* creeping stems.

  A. Flowers conspicuous.

    1. Flowers regular, i.e. radially symmetrical.

      A. Petals with long spurs   **Columbine**

Columbine, *Aquilegia.* The petals of columbines are lengthened backwards into spurs which are usually knobbed at the ends. In these, nectar is secreted which is sought by long-tongued insects and sometimes by hummingbirds. These spurs give the flowers a distinctive appearance and make them easily recognizable.

Colorado columbine, *A. caerulea,* with large blue and white, sometimes entirely white flowers, is found only at the higher altitudes in moist forests.

60. **Cliff columbine,** *A. triternata,* with red and yellow flowers, is found on the moist sandstone cliffs where there is dripping water and at the bases of the cliffs on wet ground. Its leaves are divided 3 times.

RUTH NELSON

FIGURE 60. Cliff columbine

103

61. **Golden columbine,** *A. chrysantha,* is the largest species and may be up to 4 feet tall. Its beautiful yellow flowers have long slender spurs. They may be seen along the trail going up to Weeping Rock and in other moist situations.

> B. Petals lacking spurs (but sepals with very small spurs in **mousetail**), flowers yellow, white or pinkish
> **Buttercup** and **Anemone**

Buttercup, *Ranunculus.* Buttercups are not as common in the Park as in many other areas. Local species usually have 5 petals and 5 sepals. In buttercups the sepals are separate and, except in the case of sand buttercup, they tend to fall off quite early. These sepal characters distinguish buttercups from the cinquefoils, which have their sepals united and persistent.

62. **Sagebrush buttercup,** *R. ellipticus,* is the most showy of the yellow species in Zion. Its flowers are from ½ to 1 inch across, and its sepals usually show black hairs. Its leaves are elliptical with smooth margins. **Bur-buttercup,** *R. testiculatus,* is common on disturbed soil in Zion Canyon. It is a small, erect, annual plant with small yellow flowers.

FIGURE 61. Golden columbine

LELAND ALLEN

104

FIGURE 62. Sagebrush buttercup
SCALE: 1 x 1¼

63. **Sand buttercup,** *R. juniperinus,* is a beautiful little plant which blooms very early, sometimes even in late February. It grows on the East Zion Plateau and in other sandy areas. Flowers are comparatively large, up to an inch across. The petals are at first white and the sepals pinkish. As the flowers age, the sepals enlarge and become quite red. Its bluish leaves are finely divided. **Shore buttercup,** *R. cymbalaria saximontana,* is occasionally found growing in mud at the edge of ponds or on very wet soil. It has a trailing stem and round, toothed leaves. Another buttercup occasionally found at the higher altitudes with an erect stem and an elongated cluster of achenes is *R. inamoenus.*

Anemones are rare in Zion National Park. They are characterized by collars of leaves, called *involucres,* surrounding the stem below the flowers, and long-stalked basal leaves. They have no petals, but their sepals are petal-like. *Anemone tuberosa* is a desert species found in the Park only in Coalpits Wash. It has about 10 white sepals which may be pinkish on their undersides. Another species, *A. multifida,* has been reported. **Mousetail,** *Myosurus minimus,* a small plant with narrow leaves, leafless flower stalks and an elongating receptacle holding many achenes, is sometimes found around ponds.

2. Flowers irregular, i.e. not radially symmetrical, usually blue   **Larkspur**

Larkspur, *Delphinium.* This group of plants is easily recognized because of the similarity of the wild species to cultivated varieties. Leaves are palmately divided, and the basal ones have usually partially or completely withered by flowering time. All local species are blue-flowered and somewhat similar. Flowers occur on erect stalks in what is called a *raceme* arrangement. Sepals are blue and petal-like, and the upper sepal is extended backward into a short, stout spur.

64. **Nelson larkspur,** *D. nelsonii (D. menzesii),* blooms in Zion Canyon in April, especially under oak trees just above Birch Creek. Later it may be found on the East Zion Plateau and still later on the higher plateaus such as at Lava Point. This was named for a well-known Rocky Mountain botanist, Aven Nelson.

FIGURE 63. Sand buttercup

FIGURE 64. Nelson larkspur
SCALE: 1 x ¾

65. **Desert larkspur,** *D. parishii (D. amabile),* with lighter colored flowers occurs in Coalpits Wash and on the East Zion Plateau. *D. scaposum* has practically leafless stalks, and its basal leaves are somewhat fleshy. Its flowers are a very brilliant blue. It also occurs on the East Zion Plateau. **Monkshood,** *Aconitum columbianum,* a tall plant with hooded blue flowers, has been reported for the Park.

      B. Flowers inconspicuous, small, white or green, plants 1 foot or more tall.

          1. Leaf divisions roundish, plants male or female

Meadowrue

66. **Fendler meadowrue,** *Thalictrum fendleri,* may be up to 2 feet tall. Leaves of this plant somewhat resemble the leaves of columbine or maidenhair fern. Its imperfect flowers are small, greenish or whitish.

FIGURE 65. Desert larkspur

FIGURE 65. *Flower detail*

FIGURE 66. Fendler meadowrue

SCALE: 1 x 1¼

FIGURE 67. Creeping hollygrape

They lack petals but often small sepals are present. Tassel-like groups of hanging stamens on the male plants are the most noticeable feature of meadowrue. This type of stamen is adapted for wind polination. Female plants have small clusters of green pistils which develop into flattened, asymmetrical, ribbed achenes.

2. Leaf divisions pointed **Baneberry**

Baneberry, *Actaea rubra arguta,* is a large coarse plant with very finely divided, sharp-tipped leaves. Its small white flowers are borne on a tall stalk above the leaves. They develop into round shiny berries; some plants have red berries, others white ones. Look for it in shaded canyons at the higher levels.

BARBERRY FAMILY, *Berberidaceae*

Plants of this family in Zion are shrubs with compound leaves and clusters of bright yellow fragrant flowers. The individual evergreen leaflets are spiny, like holly leaves.

67. **Creeping hollygrape,** *Berberis repens,* has stems rarely more than a foot high and pinnately compound leaves usually composed of 5 leaflets. The bright yellow flowers, which are conspicuous in early spring, are followed by clusters of bluish, edible berries. The plant grows in woods, often under oaks, in Zion's side canyons and on the plateaus. **Fremont barberry,** *B. fremontii,* a shrub up to 4 feet tall, is frequently seen on the dry slopes south and west of the Park and some-times in the lowest areas of the Park. Its leaves are bluish-green.

POPPY FAMILY, *Papaveraceae*

68. **Prickly poppy** or **thistle poppy,** *Argemone munita (A. polyan-themos),* an exceedingly prickly plant with large white flowers, occurs in the Kolob Canyons area and on the East Zion Plateau where it blooms in July.

Golden poppy, *Eschscholtzia.* Two close relatives of the California poppy, **desert golden poppy,** *E. glyptosperma,* and **little golden poppy,** *E. minutiflora,* grow in Coalpits Wash, blooming in April and May. They have small yellow flowers and finely divided, bluish leaves.

110

FIGURE 68. Prickly poppy

FUMITORY FAMILY, *Fumariaceae*

Goldensmoke, *Corydalis aurea,* is the only member of this family in the Park. It has irregular, yellow flowers about an inch long and finely cut, grayish foliage. It occurs in loose soil along partially shaded trails.

MUSTARD FAMILY, *Cruciferae*

The Latin name of this family, *Cruciferae,* is appropriately descriptive. The word means "bearing a cross," and the "crucifers," as they are commonly called, may be recognized by their 4-petaled flowers arranged in the shape of a Maltese Cross. No other group of plants has flowers of this same pattern. Usually each petal is narrowed to a slender base called a "claw." There are also 4 separate sepals which are frequently colored, sometimes like the petals, sometimes differently, and 6 stamens. The fruit is a 2-celled pod, in some genera short or rounded, but more often elongated. The shape, size and position of the pod is important in identification. (See illustrations of pods on pp. 117–122.) The flowers of many species are yellow, some are white, and some are pinkish or purple.

I. Plants with bright yellow flowers.

69. **Princesplume,** *Stanleya pinnata,* is a tall plant, up to 6 feet high, woody at base with whitish stems and large grayish leaves, the lower ones pinnately divided or compound. Flowers are yellow, and their pistils are on stalks so that they protrude from the flower giving the lower part of the raceme a fringed appearance. It blooms in spring and grows among rocks in the canyons especially on alkali soil containing the mineral *selenium,* which the plant is able to absorb. *Selenium* makes the plant poisonous to animals which might eat it.

FIGURE 69. Princesplume

70. **Wallflower**, *Erysimum capitatum*, is a showy plant with clusters of 4-petaled flowers which are bright yellow, orange or brownish. Stems are 1 to 3 feet tall, and the 4-sided pods are 2 to 4 inches long. It blooms in early spring in Zion Canyon and later at higher places.

71. **Bladderpod**, *Lesquerella intermedia*, is a low plant with silvery foliage, yellow flowers and inflated pods. A hand lens helps one see the star-shaped hairs on the stems and leaves which give them the grayish color. Flowers are from ½ to 1 inch broad, the stems 4 to 8 inches long, usually decumbent and turning up towards the tips, leaves 1 to 2 inches long, wider toward the outer end and with margins incurled. This plant is widely distributed.

Utah bladderpod, *L. utahensis*, has similar but smaller flowers, and its flat leaves are on slender stalks longer than the blades which are from ½ to ¾ inch. It grows in dry sandy areas on the plateaus. Other kinds are *L. gordonii*, which has round capsules on S-shaped stalks, and *L. rectipes*. Both of these occur in the sandy areas on the plateaus.

Twinpod, *Physaria chambersii*, is a low, compact plant with roundish silvery leaves and bright yellow flowers which may be an inch across. Except for the petals the plant is covered with small stellate hairs. The double inflated seedpod is ½ inch or more broad when fully ripe and often purplish in color. This grows on the high plateaus. A similar plant is **Newberry twinpod**, *P. newberryi*, which has smaller flowers and occurs at lower altitudes.

Draba or **whitlowgrass**, *Draba*. These are small plants with racemes of yellow or white flowers usually on leafless stalks held above basal rosettes of small leaves.

FIGURE 70. Wallflower

FIGURE 71. Bladderpod
SCALE: 1 x 1¼

72. **Early draba,** *D. asperella,* has bright yellow, 4-petaled flowers which are conspicuous compared to the size of the plant. Its leaves are covered with branched hairs; its stems are from 2 to 6 inches tall; and the smooth pods are ¼ to ½ inch long and less than half as wide. (The typical form of this plant has hairy pods, but those in Zion are smooth.) It grows on moist, shaded banks in the side canyons and on the high plateaus.

Zion draba, *D. zionis,* with pods ½ to ¾ of an inch long, is a similar but taller species. *D. reptans* is an annual species with white flowers. In dry seasons it is rare and only 2 or 3 inches tall, usually growing in the shade of shrubs. After abundant rains it becomes quite conspicuous along trails and on sandy benches, growing up to 9 inches tall and branching. It flowers in early spring. *D. rectifructa,* a hairy plant with a leafy stem, has been collected in Coalpits Wash.

II. Plants with white to yellowish, lavender, pinkish or purple flowers (for white see also under draba above).

Watercress, *Nasturtium officinale,* grows in ponds and slow clear streams in Zion Canyon. Its floating leaves make bright green beds in the ponds in early spring.

73. **Desert pepperweed,** *Lepidium fremontii,* is a rounded, bushy plant of desert-like areas, with many short clusters of small 4-petaled white flowers. Its leaves are bright green and divided into numerous narrow lobes. It has small ovate seedpods with narrow marginal wings at tips.

Mountain pepperweed, *L. montanum,* is similar. It grows in rock crevices along the Watchman Trail and in other places. Its stems are very green and smooth. The little pods are about ⅛ of an inch long. **Woolly desert pepperweed,** *L. lasiocarpum,* similar but with flattened pedicels and short, hairy pods, has been found in Coalpits Wash. **Denseflowered lepidium,** *L. densiflorum,* an annual, grows in sandy places. It has no petals, or very small ones, so its flowers are inconspicuous, but its pods are about ¼ of an inch long in dense racemes. Another pepperweed, *L. medium,* has small white petals.

116

FIGURE 72. Early draba

FIGURE 73. *Seed pod detail*

FIGURE 73. Desert pepperweed

74. **Spectaclepod**, *Dithyrea wislizenii*, is an interesting plant of sandy plains. It has several erect stems, gray wavy-toothed leaves 1 to 3 inches long, and spectacle-shaped pods about ½ inch long. Its flowers are white.

75. **Lacepod**, *Thysanocarpus amplectens*, is found in sandy areas. Its stem is erect and may be branched. The white flowers are tiny, but the circular, flat, lacy-edged pods are ⅛ to ¼ inch across and quite distinctive. **Fendler pennycress** or **wild candytuft**, *Thlaspi fendleri*, a smooth, white-flowered plant only a few inches tall, grows on the plateaus, blooming early in spring. Its pods are pointed at the base and notched at the top.

FIGURE 74.
Seed pod detail

FIGURE 74. Spectaclepod

BARBARA LUND

118

FIGURE 75. Lacepod

FIGURE 75. *Seed pod detail*

119

76. **Tall thelypody,** *Thelypodium integrifolium,* is a biennial plant which forms bright green, large, flat rosettes of smooth, entire-margined leaves the first year, from which a stalk 3 to 6 feet tall develops the second year. The plant then dies. Its inflorescence is branched into several dense racemes bearing white or pale lavender flowers on slender stalks ¼ to ⅓ inch long. The stem leaves are narrow, sessile, and entire; pods are slender, somewhat knobby, and more or less arched. "Fringes" of last year's pods are often visible on dead stalks nearby. It is found on shaded, moist hillsides.

Utah thelypody, *T. lasiophyllum,* is an annual plant, usually 1 to 3 feet tall, with wavy-toothed or pinnately lobed, stalked leaves. The upper ones are much smaller; petals are yellowish-white. The inflorescence becomes much elongated in fruit, and the slender pods hang.

Stanleyella, *Stanleyella wrightii (Thelypodium wrightii),* is a tall branched plant from 1 to 4 feet in height with short branched clusters of 4-petaled white or pinkish flowers and knobby pods 2 to 4 inches long on upcurved, slender stalks.

FIGURE 76. Tall thelypody
SCALE: 1 x ¼

FIGURE 76.
Flower detail

121

77. **Heartleaf twistflower,** *Streptanthus cordatus*, has stems 1 to 3 feet tall, thick firm bluish leaves which have heart-shaped clasping bases, and flattened pods ⅜ inch wide. Flowers have green or purplish sepals which are pinched in at the top, and yellowish or brown-purple petals. This common plant of Zion Canyon blooms in early spring.

Rockcress, *Arabis.* Plants of this group are usually erect with sessile stem leaves and flattened pods which average about 2 inches long when mature and are carried in various positions, erect, spreading, or drooping. Leaves are often grayish and rough; flowers are white, pink or purple.

78. **Perennial rockcress,** *Arabis perennans*, is one of the earliest plants to bloom in Zion Canyon, beginning sometimes in early March. It is widely distributed but inconspicuous because of its small and usually pale flowers. It often has a woody "foot" produced as the basal rosette is pushed out by new leaves in successive seasons. Leaves are wavy-toothed, and the basal ones are rough with stellate hairs. Flowers are white to purple, flower stalks are spreading, and the pods arch downwards. Stem leaves are small and scattered. This plant is found throughout Zion Canyon, on the side slopes, in side canyons, and on the plateaus.

FIGURE 77. *Seed pod detail*

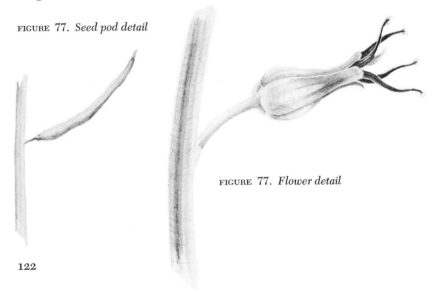

FIGURE 77. *Flower detail*

122

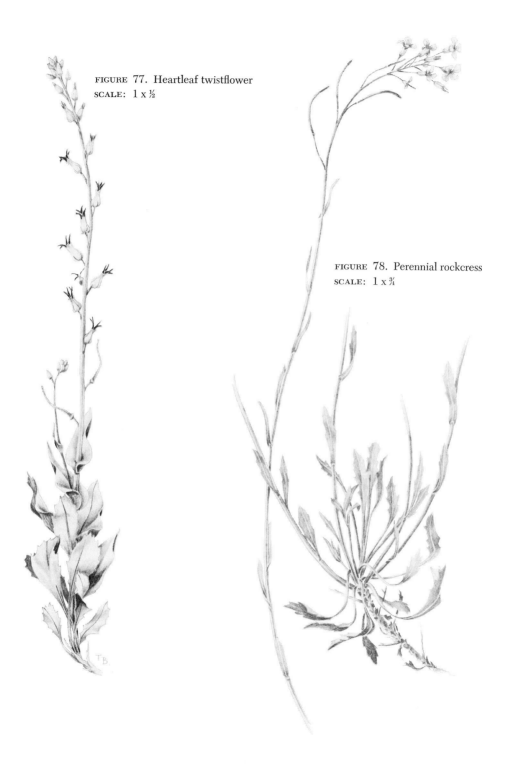

FIGURE 77. Heartleaf twistflower
SCALE: 1 x ½

FIGURE 78. Perennial rockcress
SCALE: 1 x ¾

79. **Woody-foot rockcress,** A. *lignifera,* is similar in having a woody root, but its leaves have smooth margins and are gradually reduced in size upwards. The basal ones have a finer, more dense hairiness, and the petals are usually dark purple, and the sepals are more or less covered with crimped hairs.

Fendler rockcress, A. *fendleri,* has wavy-margined leaves which are crowded at the base of the stem and diminish in size and number upwards. The basal leaves are more or less rough; pods are drooping. It occurs on the higher plateaus. A. *divaricarpa* is a green plant with thin stem leaves up to 2 inches long; the pods are thin and smooth and spread upward.

Long-beaked streptanthella, *streptanthella longirostris,* is somewhat similar to the rockcresses. It has smooth, bluish-green foliage; purple buds and yellowish petals. One pair of sepals is slightly bulged at the base. The flattened pods, which hang down, have pointed beaks and a slight swelling just back of the beak. It occurs on the East Zion Plateau, along the Sand Bench Trail, and in other sandy areas.

Squaw cabbage, *Caulanthus crassicaulis,* is a stout, single-stemmed, unbranched plant 1 to 3 feet tall, with smooth, pale greenish-blue leaves which are reduced in size upwards. The stem is conspicuously inflated. The color of the 4 purplish sepals is almost concealed by their white hairiness, and the purple, ½ inch long petals have white margins. This is a desert plant which occurs in Zion in the Petrified Forest region. It was cooked and eaten by the Indians of the area.

80. **Chorispora,** *Chorispora tenella,* is conspicuous in early spring on soil where the native vegetation has been destroyed. It has 4-petaled purple flowers.

CAPER FAMILY, *Capparidaceae*

This is a family related to the mustard family, having 4-petaled flowers. They provide very good bee pasture.

81. **Yellow beeplant** or **spiderflower,** *Cleome lutea,* is a plant up to 2 feet tall having palmately compound leaves with 3 to 5 leaflets and yellow 4-petaled flowers. The flowers have a spidery effect due to the

FIGURE 79. Woody-foot rockcress

FIGURE 80. Chorispora, *flowers purple*
SCALE: 1 x ¾

FIGURE 82. Stonecrop

long thread-like stamen stalks which extend beyond the petals; the anthers at the tip of each stalk are coiled. This grows on sandy soil throughout the area. **Rocky Mountain beeplant,** *Cleome serrulata,* is similar but has purple or rose flowers. The latter occurs along the Mount Carmel Road and only occasionally within the Park.

ORPINE FAMILY, *Crassulaceae*

82. **Stonecrop,** *Sedum lanceolatum (S. stenopetalum),* has small rosettes of smooth, cylindrical, juicy leaves and erect stalks a few inches tall, bearing recurved clusters of flowers with 5 (or sometimes 4) pointed yellow petals. It is found on sunny rocks along the West Rim Trail and in other rocky places. **Weak-stemmed stonecrop,** *S. debile,* is a fragile plant with blunt, rounded, opposite, sessile leaves and yellow flowers; it is rare in the Park but is sometimes found in damp, shaded situations.

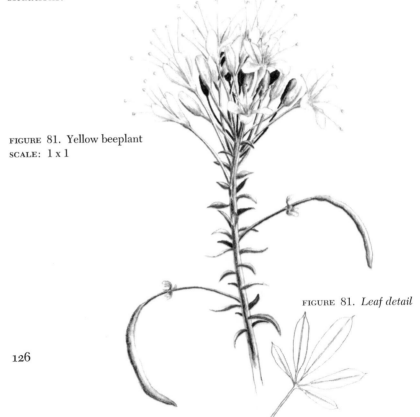

FIGURE 81. Yellow beeplant
SCALE: 1 x 1

FIGURE 81. *Leaf detail*

126

The plants of this family are perennials; they may be shrubs or herbs; leaves are simple (i.e. not made up of separate leaflets, see p. 308), but they may be variously lobed or toothed. There are usually 5 petals, occasionally 4. These and the stamens are inserted on the rim of a cup-like structure, the calyx tube, surrounding the ovary and more or less attached to it.

I. Woody plants.

　　A. Bark shredding; leaves opposite; fruits dry pods.

Cliff jamesia, *Jamesia americana*, is a shrub with opposite, strongly veined leaves and clusters of white flowers about ½ to nearly 1 inch wide. The petals are somewhat hairy inside. It grows in rock crevices of the Upper Sonoran and Transition Zones. In autumn the leaves turn a beautiful rose color. The plant was named for Dr. Edwin James, the botanist who accompanied Major Long on his exploring trip to the Rocky Mountains in 1820. Dr. James and two companions were the first people to climb Pikes Peak, where they collected many plants new to science, especially alpine species.

83. **Littleleaf mock orange**, *Philadelphus microphyllus*, is a shrub with reddish-brown or tan bark which shreds and comes off in strips, leaving the stems striped. The leaves are from ½ to 1½ inches long, ovate or lanceolate. The white to cream-colored flowers are from ½ to nearly 1 inch wide. This shrub grows in rock crevices and at the bases of cliffs in the canyons. A variety with even smaller leaves which grows in dry canyons is *P. microphyllus occidentalis*.

　　B. Bark not shredding, leaves alternate, fruits juicy berries.

84. **Squaw currant** or **wax currant**, *Ribes cereum*, is a much-branched shrub with rounded, 3 to 5-lobed, sticky leaves which are ½ to 1½ inch wide. The pinkish flowers hang down and are also sticky. The fruits are round, red, sticky berries which are eaten by birds and chipmunks but have an insipid flavor. This shrub grows on the high plateaus.

FIGURE 83. Littleleaf mock-orange
SCALE: 1 x 1

FIGURE 84. Squaw currant
SCALE: 1 x ¾

Golden currant, *R. aureum,* a shrub with long-tubed yellow, or sometimes reddish, flowers and smooth, lobed leaves, grows in the Watchman Campground. The shrub is native in Utah, but probably the ones found here were planted by early settlers. In Utah the berries are usually golden to reddish or black and of good flavor.

    II. Herbaceous plants, leaves mostly basal.

        A. Leaves with smooth margins, flowers solitary.

Small flower parnassia, *Parnassia parviflora,* has a rosette of oval or ovate leaves and a slender stalk bearing one ovate leaf just below the middle and a single white-petaled flower ½ to 1 inch broad. This grows on moist ground or in swamps on the high plateaus.

        B. Leaves with lobed or toothed margins, flowers in open clusters.

    85. **Alumroot,** *Heuchera versicolor,* is a plant with a basal rosette of roundish, lobed leaves and slender stalks from 8 to 14 inches tall, bearing open clusters of pinkish flowers from which the stamens protrude. The plants grow on cliffs and in rock crevices in shaded, moist places. There are conspicuous hairs on the leaf stalks and sometimes on the leaves. **Red alumroot,** *H. rubescens,* is a similar plant which is slightly less hairy and more sticky. It grows in similar locations. *H. parvifolia,* a rare plant in this area, grows on moist, shaded banks at the higher altitudes.

    86. **Woodland star,** *Lithophragma tenella,* is a dainty, slender plant with palmately lobed and much-divided basal leaves and finely cleft white or pinkish petals. There are often little bulblets at the base of the stem among the leaf bases. This occurs on wooded plateau areas, especially under ponderosa pines. *L. bulbifera* is a similar plant. Some of its flowers are replaced by tiny reddish bulbs. Leaves are less finely divided. It occurs in moist, mossy places on the plateaus.

        C. Leaves not lobed but pointed, flowers in dense clusters.

Diamondleaf saxifrage, *Saxifraga rhomboidea,* is a small, rare plant with a basal rosette of pointed leaves and a slender stalk bearing a dense cluster of white flowers. This has been found growing on a mossy bank just below the edge of the East Rim.

FIGURE 85. Alumroot
SCALE: 1 x 1

FIGURE 86. Woodlandstar
SCALE: 1 x 1½

131

This plant group resembles the buttercup family in its variability. In general its flowers have 5 separate petals which, with the many stamens, are attached to a saucer or cup-like structure formed by the united base of the 5 sepals. The character of united sepals plus this position of the petals and stamens differentiates these plants from the buttercups. The family contains many shrubs. Most of its species growing in Zion National Park are woody.

> I. Species with woody stems (in the case of rock spiraea the stems are very low and mat-like).

> A. Stems prickly.

Woods wild rose, *Rosa woodsii,* has prickly stems, compound leaves with 5 to 7 leaflets which are sharply toothed, and pink flowers about 2 inches across. It has a red, berry-like fruit called a "hip." There may be one or two other species in the Park. The kinds of wild roses are very similar and hard to distinguish but easily recognized as roses.

Whitebark raspberry or **blackcap,** *Rubus leucodermis,* is a weak-stemmed, prickly shrub found growing in rocky places or among other bushes. Its leaves have from 3 to 5 toothed leaflets; the 5-petaled flowers are white. The ripe fruit is dark purple or black, juicy and sweet.

> B. Stems not prickly.

> > 1. Flowers yellow (or almost white in Cowania).

87. **Cliffrose** or **cowania,** *Cowania stansburyana,* is a stout shrub with shreddy bark and small (not over 1 inch long), pinnately lobed leaves which are white beneath. The flowers are light yellow when first open but may become whitish. They have 5 rounded petals and numerous yellow stamens. The shrubs in full bloom are handsome and picturesque. They often become quite old and have a weatherbeaten appearance. The few pistils have long plumose styles which become 2 to 3 inches long in fruit. It occurs on dry rocky slopes and mesas throughout the Sonoran Zones.

FIGURE 87. Cliffrose, *petals pale yellow*

Antelope bitterbrush, *Purshia tridentata*, is quite similar to cliffrose as to flowers and leaves but is a much lower shrub. The main difference is that instead of many long-tailed achenes this has 1 or 2 pistils which become large achenes with stout beaks. This plant is rare in Zion Canyon, but it is an important southwestern Utah browse plant for sheep, cattle and deer. It may be found at altitudes from 4,000 to 7,000 feet, but it is most common among pines on the plateaus.

88. **Blackbrush,** *Coleogyne ramosissimum,* is a shrub of the Lower Sonoran Zone which occurs only at the southern end of the Park and along the Watchman Trail. It has opposite branching and small narrow leaves which are dark green; the flowers are small with 4 yellowish sepals, usually no petals. The leaves are crowded, and the branchlets often become spine-tipped. The shrubs have a very dark aspect during most of the year, but when the new leaves come out in the spring they are a lovely soft green.

2. Flowers white, cream-colored or pinkish.

89. **Utah serviceberry,** *Amelanchier utahensis,* is one of the most common shrubs on the slopes of Zion Canyon. These shrubs, 4 to 10 feet tall, become covered with clusters of small white flowers in early April. Their leaves are round. They have small dry berry-like fruits.

FIGURE 88. Blackbrush

J. L. CRAWFORD

134

FIGURE 89. Utah serviceberry
SCALE: 1 x 1¼

90. **Saskatoon serviceberry,** *A. alnifolia,* is usually taller with larger leaves, toothed around the upper portion, and clusters of attractive white flowers. Its fruit is sweet and edible, much sought after by animals and used by Indians and by pioneers for pies and preserves. It grows in the cool canyons among trees and on the higher plateaus.

91. **Apacheplume,** *Fallugia paradoxa,* is a white-barked shrub with arching branches and small pinnately-lobed leaves. Its white flowers are 1 to 2 inches across, and there are 5 pointed calyx lobes with 5 additional alternating small bractlets. There are many stamens and pistils, and the plumose styles, which may become up to 2 inches long, turn rose or purplish at maturity. It occurs in dry washes and on rocky slopes.

Squawapple, *Peraphyllum ramosissimum,* is a shrub which has rigid gray-barked branches and clustered leaves which are broadest and rounded at the outer end. It has pink and white crabapple-like blossoms, and the fruits are small, yellowish, bitter apples. It is rare on the floor of Zion Canyon but abundant on some of the higher plateaus.

FIGURE 90. Saskatoon serviceberry
SCALE: 1 x 1

136

FIGURE 91. Apache plume, *in fruit*

92. **Desert peachbrush** or **desert almond,** *Prunus fasciculata,* is a small rigidly branched shrub with clustered leaves and green or pinkish flowers which are followed by hairy, dry, almond-shaped fruits. It occurs near the mouth of Zion Canyon and in other desert areas.

93. **Western chokecherry,** *Prunus virginiana melanocarpa,* is a common shrub on the higher plateaus. Its smooth, shiny leaves are from 2 to 5 inches long, usually widest toward the outer end, with long tapering tips. **Mountain spray,** *Holodiscus dumosus,* has somewhat pyramid-shaped flower clusters of creamy white which begin to turn pinkish or rusty as they age. The leaves, ½ to 2½ inches long, are wedge-shaped at base with a few teeth on each side. Underneath they are hairy and often whitish. This grows on rocky slopes in the upper parts of the side canyons and on the plateaus.

FIGURE 92. Desert peachbrush, *in fruit*

FIGURE 93. Western chokecherry

FIGURE 93. *Flower detail*

Rockmat or **rockspiraea**, *Petrophytum caespitosum*, is a small low plant with a woody, prostrate stem and many little rosettes of grayish leaves which form mats on rock surfaces. The erect stalks, 3 to 5 inches tall, are leafless with compact clusters of small white flowers. The mat is anchored by one or more cord-like woody stems which penetrate a rock crevice.

3. Flowers inconspicuous, small, yellowish or brownish.

94. **Littleleaf mountain-mahogany,** *Cercocarpus intricatus*, is a gray-barked shrub with rigid branches and many narrow leaves with inrolled edges. Leaves are evergreen and the flowers very small and inconspicuous. Many of the shrubs which dot the slickrock belong to this species. They are abundant along the Canyon Overlook Trail, especially as you climb the stairway. **Curlleaf mountain-mahogany,** *C. ledifiolius*, has wider leaves, grows at higher altitudes, and is much less common. **Alderleaf mountain-mahogany,** *C. montanus*, has wider, flat leaves which it loses in winter. It occurs on the high plateaus and sometimes becomes 8 to 10 feet tall.

II. Species with herbaceous (non-woody) stems.

Ivesia, *Ivesia sabulosa*, is a plant of sandstone crevices, usually found on the slickrock. It has long, narrow, compound leaves made up of many tiny, crowded leaflets. The yellowish flowers have 5 rounded petals. The 5-pointed flower-tube, or calyx, has 5 additional narrow bractlets.

95. **Leafy cinquefoil,** *Potentilla fissa*, is a leafy plant 6 to 14 inches tall with light yellow, 5 petaled flowers about an inch across. Its leaves are pinnately compound with several toothed leaflets, the terminal one being the largest. It grows in wooded areas of the plateaus.

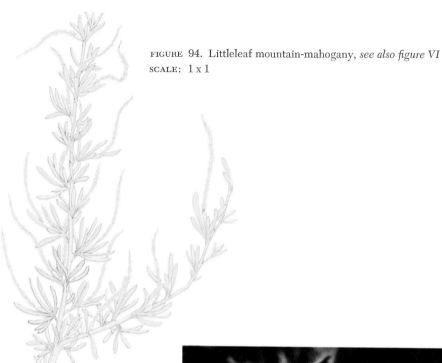

FIGURE 94. Littleleaf mountain-mahogany, *see also figure VI*
SCALE: 1 x 1

FIGURE 95. Leafy cinquefoil

141

PEA FAMILY, *Leguminosae*

Most plants of this family are easily recognized by the irregular, sweet pea type flower (see fig. 17, p. 315). In most kinds there are 5 petals which are separate except for the 2 lower ones, which may be more or less united to form a boat-shaped *keel*. The sepals are united. In most of the species 9 of the 10 stamens have their stalks joined together. Nearly all members have compound leaves. The leaflets may be either palmately or pinnately arranged. The typical fruit is called a *legume* and usually resembles a pea or bean pod. Some members of this family, such as locusts, are trees, others are shrubs, and many are annual or perennial herbs. Garden peas and beans belong in this family.

I. Trees or shrubs with pinnately compound leaves.

Honey mesquite, *Prosopis juliflora (P. glandulosa)*, is a small thorny tree or shrub with crooked branches and very deep roots. It has bright green hanging leaves of numerous narrow leaflets. Its brown flat pods, 3 to 6 inches long and constricted between the seeds, are an important food for animals as well as Indians, who grind them into a sweet meal. It occurs only in washes along the southern edge of the Park. (This has sometimes been classified in the Mimosa family.)

96. **New Mexico locust,** *Robinia neomexicana*, is a large or low shrub, sometimes a small bushy tree, covered with short spines and bearing clusters of light pink blossoms in late May. It occurs along the lower slopes of Zion Canyon and is particularly noticeable around the Visitor Center. **Black locust,** *R. pseudoacacia*, was planted here by early settlers and persists in a few places.

FIGURE 96. New Mexico locust

97. **Desert beauty** or **indigo bush**, *Dalea fremontii*, is a thorny desert shrub blooming in May with clusters of brilliant blue flowers, found along the southern edge of the Park.

II. Herbs with 3 to 5 leaflets closely grouped.

A. Leaflets dotted with tiny black dots. It may be necessary to use a hand lens to see these.

98. **Prairieclover**, *Petalostemon searlesii*, is a plant with tall flower stalks bearing dense, elongated clusters of handsome purple flowers always showing their bright orange anthers. It grows in the Lower Sonoran Zone. **Scurfpea** or **desert beaverbread**, *Psoralea castorea*, is a low plant with grayish, palmately compound leaves somewhat resembling lupine leaves. It has a short spike of bluish flowers and very short, beaked pods. This grows in sandy areas at low altitudes, especially in the Petrified Forest region. Two species with white flowers are **lemon scurfpea**, *P. lanceolata*, and **Bigelow scurfpea**, *P. tenuiflora bigelovii*, with narrower leaflets, which, because of its spreading rootstock, often covers large areas. These occur at low altitudes in the Park.

Licorice, *Glycyrrhiza lepidota*, is a plant 1 to 3 feet tall with short clusters of pale yellowish flowers. The foliage and calyxes are somewhat sticky; pods are prickly and form a bur-like cluster. It infrequently occurs near the Virgin River.

B. Leaflets not dotted.

Clover, *Trifolium*. Native plants have recognizable clover-type leaves of 3 leaflets and compact flower heads.

99. **Utah clover**, *T. kingii* (*T. macilentum*), has rose-colored heads about an inch long. Individual flowers are ½ inch long and reflexed. Both heads and leaves are on long stalks. The leaflets are marked like those of common red clover, but those of the lower leaves are oval and

FIGURE 97. Desert beauty

FIGURE 98. Prairieclover

145

those of the upper ones are narrower and long-pointed. It grows on moist banks and ledges in shaded canyons. **Rusby clover,** *T. longipes pygmaeum,* has whitish flowers which turn brown and become reflexed as they fade. It occurs in open forest or meadows of the Transition Zone.

Goldenpea, *Thermopsis pinetorum* or *T. montana,* is found on the plateaus. It is a plant 1 to 2 feet tall with 3 leaflets, showy yellow flowers in June, and bean-like pods. It has sometimes been called "false lupine."

Deerclover, *Lotus,* is a group of plants having yellow sweet pea-like flowers which turn orange or reddish so that usually both colors are present.

100. **Longbract deerclover,** *L. longibracteatus,* is the most commonly seen. It usually has several spreading stems. The leaflets are silvery. It grows in rocky or sandy areas throughout the Park. **Utah deerclover,**

FIGURE 99. Utah clover
SCALE: 1 x 1

146

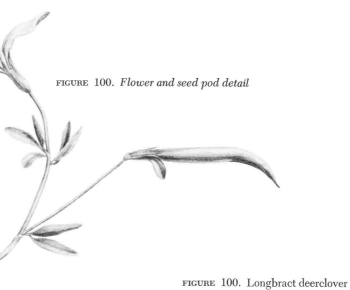

FIGURE 100. *Flower and seed pod detail*

FIGURE 100. Longbract deerclover

147

L. utahensis and *L. rigidus*, are similar but taller and more erect. They grow at the higher altitudes and have their flowers in clusters.

III. Herbs with 5 to many leaflets.

   A. Plants with pinnate leaves and tendrils or bristles at the tips of leaves.

101. **Zion sweetpea,** *Lathyrus zionis,* is a beautiful plant with brilliant flowers. The large broad banner is a rich rose-purple, the center of the flower paler. Its narrow, strongly veined leaflets are sharply pointed. This grows on banks in Zion Canyon and along the Emerald Pools Trail. **Aspen sweetpea,** *L. leucanthus,* has white or cream-colored flowers which turn brown as they fade. Its leaflets are broad below the middle, then taper to end in a short, small, sharp tip. This plant has tendrils but seldom climbs. **American vetch,** *Vicia americana*, is a similar plant with smaller blue or purplish flowers in clusters of from 4 to 9. Its leaflets are more or less oval. It clings to bushes or trees with its slender tendrils and is somewhat climbing. **Slim vetch,** *V. exigua,* has very narrow, pointed leaflets less than an inch long and whitish or bluish flowers about ¼ inch long, only 1 or 2 together. This is found at low altitudes in Zion Canyon.

   B. Plants with pinnate leaves but no tendrils.

Milkvetch, *Astragalus.* This is a large genus of plants in Zion National Park. The Park has at least 12 different kinds. Many are so similar they are hard to distinguish except on technical botanical characteristics, but the group is easy to recognize. They have pinnately compound leaves, often covered with silvery hairs. There are many white to purple, pea-like flowers arranged in racemes (see fig. 20, p. 316). The keel of the flower has a blunt tip. The plants often grow on alkali soil and some absorb the mineral *selenium.* This may make them poisonous to animals. As a result they are sometimes called "poisonweeds" or "locoweeds." Pods are often conspicuous and usually necessary for accurate identification. The most conspicuous and commonly seen species are described, and the others are listed.

FIGURE 101. Zion sweetpea

148

102. **Rattleweed milkvetch** or **straightstem poisonweed**, *A. praelongus (A. sabulosus)*, is a tall branching plant with cream-colored flowers and large, thick, woody pods. These dry and become "rattles" which hang on the dry stems. The plant is common in the Park and conspicuous along the Scenic Canyon Drive in late May when in flower. Another species with white or cream-colored (or sometimes light blue) flowers is *A. flavus candicans* which forms spreading clumps with many erect flower stalks. It grows in desert-like areas of the Lower Sonoran Zone as at the Petrified Forest.

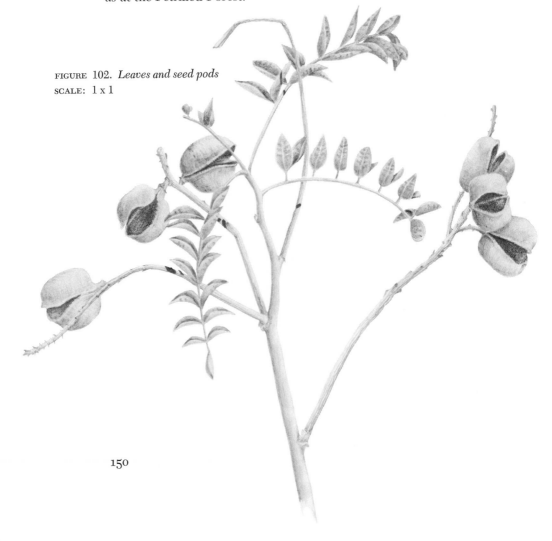

FIGURE 102. *Leaves and seed pods*
SCALE: 1 x 1

FIGURE 102. Rattleweed, *flowers cream white*

103. **Zion milkvetch,** A. *zionis,* is one of the earliest conspicuous spring flowers to bloom in Zion Canyon. Its blossoms are a handsome purple set off by the silvery foliage. It forms low clumps on rocky slopes throughout the canyon. The flowers turn blue as they age. Its pods are rather hairy, somewhat inflated, usually mottled, and become nearly 1 inch long. Similar species are: **Silverleafed milkvetch,** A. *argophyllus panguicensis,* A. *marianus,* which grows on the high plateaus, and A. *amphioxys.* **Newberry milkvetch,** A. *newberryi,* is a low, compact, short-stemmed, silvery plant which grows on red sand-clay slopes in the Lower Sonoran Zone. It has pinkish-purple flowers and curved pods about ½ inch long which are densely covered with long white hairs. **Thompson milkvetch,** A. *thompsonae (A. molissimus thompsonae),* is a silvery plant with many hairy leaflets and flower stalks up to a foot tall. The flowers are purple, and the curved pods, not quite an inch long, are densely covered with tangled white hairs. This was first collected by and named for Mrs. Thompson (see ref. under no. 44, p. 82). A. *minthorniae* or A. *lentiginosus palens,* is a desert plant 1 to 2 feet tall with pale flowers and inch-long pods slightly curved upwards.

Easter egg milkvetch, A. *oophorus,* is conspicuous in fruit, with egg-shaped, inflated pods which are usually covered with reddish markings. The foliage is smooth and green and the flowers cream-colored. It occurs in semi-shaded areas on the plateaus.

Rush-leaved milkvetch, A. *convallarius,* with slender green stems and very narrow leaves, has been found at the Petrified Forest area. A. *miser,* with leaves made up of narrow leaflets which overtop the short clusters of white or pale lilac flowers, occurs on dry sandy ridges of the Kolob Canyons area. This plant contains *miserotoxin* and is very poisonous to cattle. **Nuttall milkvetch,** A. *nuttallianus,* is an annual species with low-spreading stems and blue and white flowers about ¼ inch long which grows on dry plains and slopes in the lower canyon.

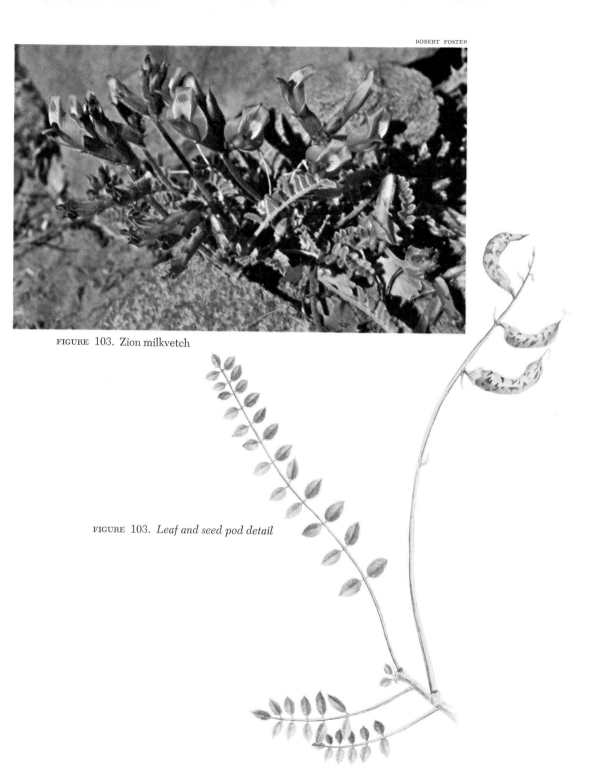

FIGURE 103. Zion milkvetch

FIGURE 103. *Leaf and seed pod detail*

104. **Thompson peteria**, *Peteria thompsonae*, is quite similar in general appearance to some of the milkvetches. It may be recognized by the pair of small, sharp spines at the base of each leaf. There are many oval or obovate leaflets from ¼ to ½ inch in length and often slightly notched at the tip. There is a long spike of flowers, whitish or yellowish and sometimes purple-tipped. This is common at the lower end of Zion Canyon. (See ref. to Mrs. Thompson, p. 82.)

C. Plants with palmate leaves.

Lupine, *Lupinus*. These plants have a distinctive character in their leaves which makes them easy to recognize. These leaves are always palmately compound with from 5 to 9 leaflets which are usually narrowed towards the end attached to the leaf stalk. The pink to blue flowers are in racemes. The plants are more or less hairy.

105. **Yelloweye lupine**, *L. flavoculatus*, is a small annual desert plant with hairy leaves and short racemes of bright blue flowers, each one having a yellow spot on the banner. It grows in sandy areas at low elevations in the Park. **Orcutt lupine**, *L. concinnus orcuttii,* is another desert plant which has pinkish flowers. It starts to bloom when its stem

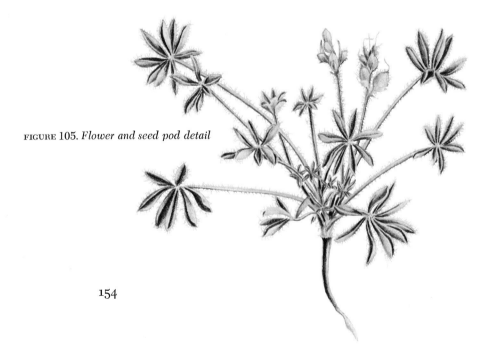

FIGURE 105. *Flower and seed pod detail*

154

FIGURE 104. Thompson peteria

FIGURE 105. Yelloweye lupine

is very short but develops longer, branched stems later in the season. The leaves may have from 5 to 9 leaflets which are covered with silky hairs. It occurs in sandy areas, such as along the Sand Bench Trail.

106. **Columbian lupine,** *L. latifolius columbianus,* is one of the handsomest plants in the Park. This has green leaves and grows 2 to 3 feet tall. By flowering time the basal leaves have usually withered. The flowering racemes may be from 6 to 12 inches long, with numerous pink-purple flowers which have a dark reddish-purple spot on the banner. It grows from a spreading underground rootstock, so it often occurs in large clumps. It is found along streams and in open, moist woods in the Upper Sonoran Zone. **Silky lupine,** *L. sericeus,* is a tall silvery species with blue or white flowers which occurs on the plateaus. There is a handsome, tall lupine which grows among sagebrush along the road to the Kolob Reservoir just outside the Park across from Lee Valley. It has cream-white flowers with brown spots on the banners and has been identified as a hybrid between *L. jonesii* and *L. sericeus huffmanii.*

GERANIUM FAMILY, *Geraniaceae*

This family is best known for the cultivated "geraniums" which are plants of the genus *Pelargonium.* Native kinds have similar long-pointed seed capsules from which some species take the name of "cranesbill" or "storksbill." The **wild geranium,** *Geranium caespitosum,* of Zion is a rare plant with erect or sometimes horizontal and more or less zigzag stems. It has 5-petaled pink or rose-purple flowers and 10 stamens. Its palmate leaves have 3 or 5 lobes with toothed margins.

FIGURE 106. Columbian lupine

ROBERT FOSTER

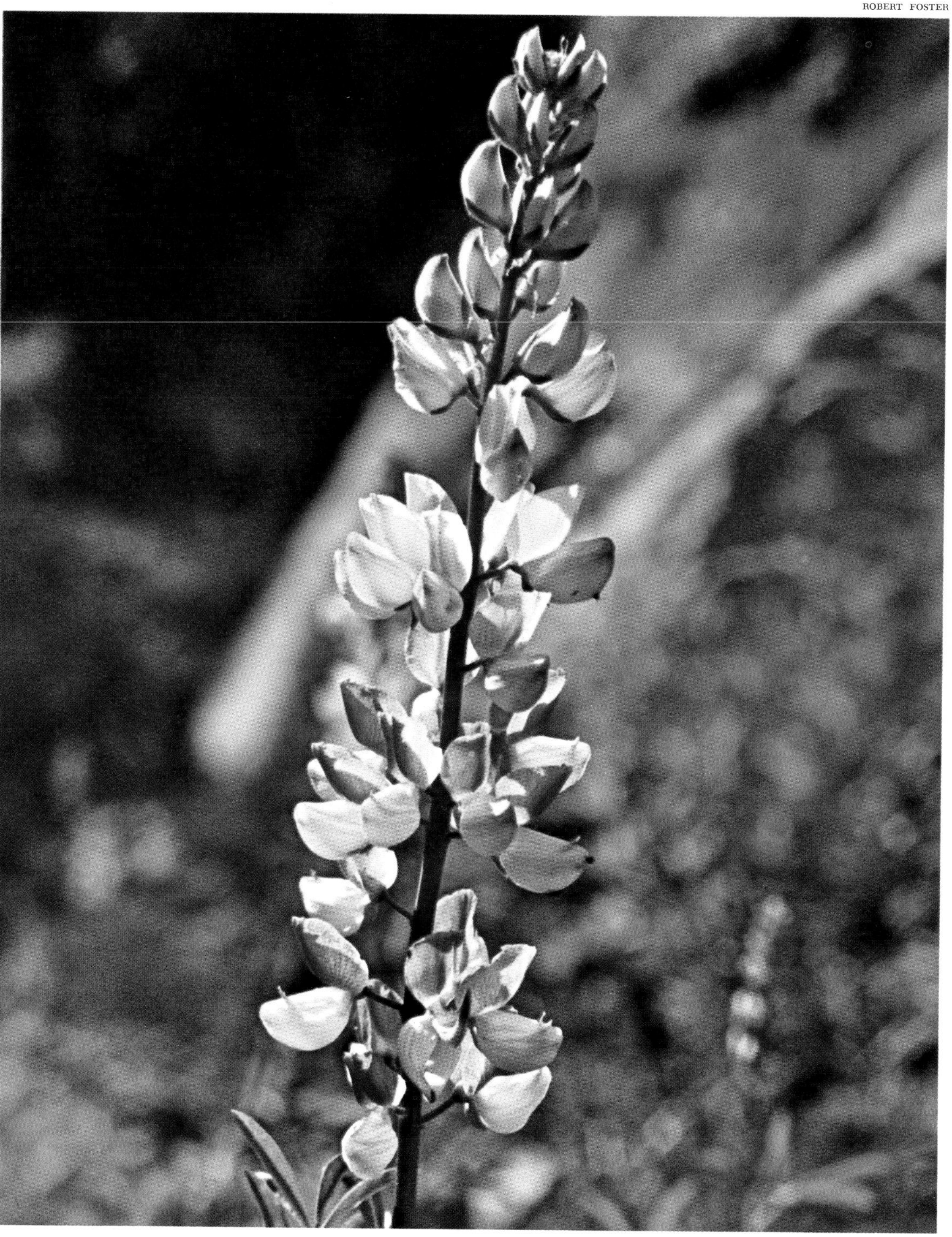

FIGURE 107. Filaree

107. **Filaree** or **alfilaria,** *Erodium cicutarium,* is a low, annual, widely distributed plant with small, bright purple flowers and irregularly pinnately lobed or toothed leaves. It begins to bloom very early on roadsides, old fields and areas of disturbed soil. It is a valuable forage plant which was introduced years ago from the Mediterranean region.

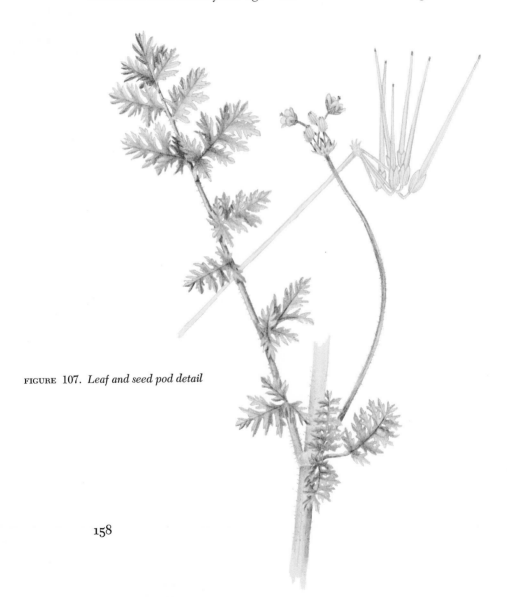

FIGURE 107. *Leaf and seed pod detail*

158

FLAX FAMILY, *Linaceae*

The flowers of this family have 5 spearate, ephemeral petals, 5 stamens, and round seed capsules.

108. **Lewis flax**, *Linum lewisii*, has stems 10 to 30 inches tall which spread upward from the crown. They are lined with narrow, inch-long leaves. The delicate blue petals usually drop off by noon to be replaced by new unfolding buds the next day. This plant was named for Meriwether Lewis (see p. 98). It is closely related to the cultivated flax from which linen thread and linseed oil are produced.

109. **Yellow flax**, *L. aristatum*, is an annual, much-branched plant of sandy areas, having few, small, sharp-pointed leaves. Its yellow petals drop within a few hours.

FIGURE 108. Lewis flax

RUTH NELSON

FIGURE 109. Yellow flax
SCALE: 1 x 1

161

CALTROP FAMILY, *Zygophyllaceae*

Creosote bush, *Larrea divaricata,* is a much-branched shrub up to 6 feet tall, with small yellowish-green leaves which appear as if varnished. It is an indicator of the Lower Sonoran Zone and occurs in Zion National Park only in Coalpits Wash, along the lower part of the Watchman Trail, and in the lower Parunuweap Canyon. It is very common on dry hillsides south of the Park and is attractive when covered with its interesting yellow flowers, which are followed by round fuzzy pods. Another member of this family is the introduced plant called **Puncture-vine,** *Tribulus terrestris,* which grows on disturbed ground flat to the earth, with pale yellow flowers and hard fruits bearing 3 stout spines.

PARADISE TREE FAMILY, *Simaroubaceae*

Ailanthus or **paradise tree,** *Ailanthus altissima,* is a vigorous tree growing along the highway near the South Entrance. This tree, a native of China, was originally planted by the early pioneers and has persisted, spreading by suckers from underground stems. It has thick twigs and long, pinnately compound leaves.

SPURGE FAMILY, *Euphorbiaceae*

This is one of the few plant families having a milky juice. Its flowers are very inconspicuous, but in some species, as in the cultivated poinsettia, these are surrounded by modified leaves which may be showy, or by petal-like appendages. Native species are inconspicuous and grow mostly on sandy soil.

110. **Carpetweed,** *Euphorbia albomarginata,* is a small, smooth, spreading plant which grows flat on the ground. It has opposite, roundish or ovate leaves less than ½ inch long, usually unequal at the base. Its tiny flowers are edged with white borders. **Fendler carpetweed,** *E. fendleri,* is similar except it lacks the conspicuous white edging, is sometimes a little more erect, and sometimes the whole plant has a reddish tinge. Another similar species in this group is *E. ocellata arenicola.* *E. revoluta* is an erect plant. **Stout spurge,** *Euphorbia robusta,* is a

162

FIGURE 110. Carpetweed

smooth plant with erect stems and numerous oblong to nearly heart-shaped, sessile stem leaves. Its inconspicuous greenish flowers are in a more or less umbellate inflorescence, and the 3-lobed fruits are on short, curved stalks. It occurs in sandy places on the plateaus. **California croton,** *Croton californicus,* is a grayish, branched plant up to 3 feet tall, with oblong leaves and milky juice, which grows on the floor of Zion Canyon in sandy places.

SUMAC FAMILY, *Anacardiaceae*

These are shrubby plants with compound or lobed leaves which turn beautiful shades of red in autumn.

111. **Squawbush** or **threeleaf sumac,** *Rhus trilobata,* is a common shrub of hillsides and canyons in the Upper Sonoran and Transition Zones. It may have 3-lobed or thrice-compound leaves which are more or less toothed. Its small yellowish flowers in short compact clusters begin to bloom before the leaves come out. The leaves are reddish at first, but later become bright green and shiny; fruits are small, sticky, fuzzy, red berries which have an acid flavor and are sometimes used to make a drink like lemonade. They are also eaten by animals. The shrubs are browsed, and the long slender shoots are used by Indian women for basketry. The variety with simple leaves has been called **Utah squaw-bush,** *R. trilobata simplicifolia,* but all intermediates in leaf form may be found.

112. **Smooth sumac,** *R. glabra,* with long, pinnately compound leaves and clusters of red, sticky berries, occurs on some moist canyon slopes like those near the base of the West Rim Trail.

Poison ivy, *R. radicans,* has compound leaves of 3 shiny, pointed leaflets and clusters of yellowish or whitish berries. It is sometimes found on moist, shaded banks but is not common.

FIGURE 111. Utah squawbush, *leaf detail*

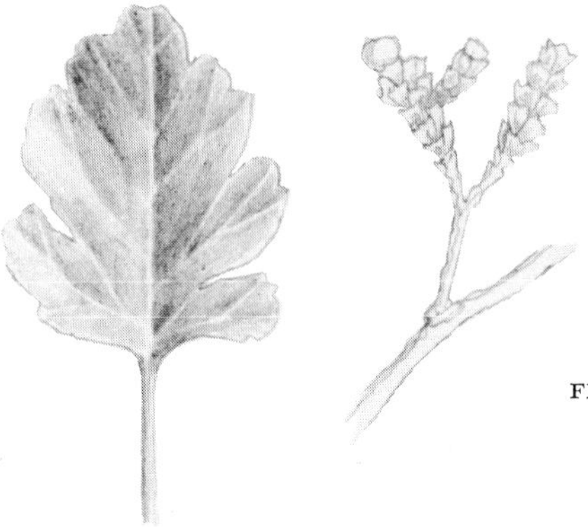

FIGURE 111. Squawbush,
leaves and flowers

FIGURE 112. Smooth sumac leaf
SCALE: 1 x 1¼

165

113. **Myrtle pachystima** or **mountain-lover,** *Pachystima myrsinites,* is the only local representative of this family. It is a low, somewhat trailing shrub with small, glossy, evergreen leaves oppositely arranged, and small 4-petaled, reddish-green flowers in the leaf axils. It usually grows in moist, shaded areas on the plateaus.

MAPLE FAMILY, *Aceraceae*

This is a family of trees or large shrubs usually having lobed leaves and winged seeds in the characteristic maple-key form.

114. **Bigtooth maple,** *Acer grandidentatum,* is a small tree frequently found on the north-facing slopes of the side canyons and in moist places on the plateaus. Its leaves are about 3 inches wide, 3 to 5-lobed, and turn beautiful shades of red in fall. **Rocky Mountain maple,** *A. glabrum,* is a shrub with small, 3-lobed or 3-parted leaves, occasionally found on the plateaus. Its winter twigs and buds are red. **Boxelder,** *A. negundo*

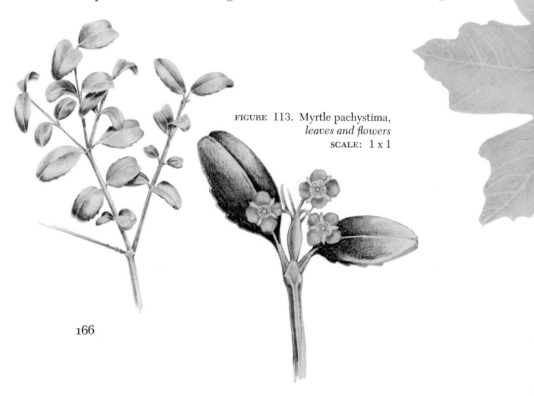

FIGURE 113. Myrtle pachystima,
leaves and flowers
SCALE: 1 x 1

166

FIGURE 114. *Leaf and fruit detail*

FIGURE 114. Bigtooth maple, *autumn color*

interior, is a tree up to 40 feet in height, common on the canyon floor and in the side canyons. Its leaves are compound of 3 to 5-lobed leaflets, and its flowers and seeds occur in long tassel-like clusters. Its young twigs are green.

BUCKTHORN FAMILY, *Rhamnaceae*

Fendler ceanothus or **buckbrush,** *Ceanothus fendleri,* is a low spiny shrub of the plateaus, usually in pine forests. Its leaves have 3 veins, and it has short clusters of dainty white flowers. It is much browsed by deer and cattle. *C. martini,* which has no spines, has been reported for the Park. *C. greggii,* a rigid shrub with stout, opposite branches, occurs on dry mountainsides south and west of Zion, approaching the Park at the Kolob Canyons Entrance.

GRAPE FAMILY, *Vitaceae*

115. **Canyon wild grape,** *Vitis arizonica,* is abundant on the floor of Zion Canyon and in the lower parts of the side canyons. This woody vine climbs trees and makes canopies over shrubs. It has large, heart-shaped, lobed leaves and clusters of small, dark, edible berries. Wild grapes are useful in several ways. The berries make excellent jelly and grape juice and were used by the Indians and pioneers. The leaves when chewed relieve thirst, and the vines are valuable for erosion control. Varieties of cultivated grapes have persisted in places on the canyon floor since the days of the pioneers.

MALLOW FAMILY, *Malvaceae*

This is the family to which hollyhocks, hibiscus, cotton and okra belong. Its flowers have 5 petals more or less united at base and many stamens which are joined into a "column" around the several-celled pistil. Most of the species have a mucilaginous juice. The sticky root of one was used to make the original "marshmallow" candy.

FIGURE 115. Canyon wild grape
SCALE: 1 x 1

169

116. **Gooseberryleaf globemallow,** *Sphaeralcea grossulariaefolia,* is the common species found blooming in May and early June about the Visitor Center and on the lower slopes of the canyon walls. It is a silvery plant with stems often in clusters, 1 to 2 feet tall. The salmon-pink or pale red, yellow-centered flowers are in loose, elongated clusters; leaves are conspicuously veined and deeply divided into 3 or 5 lobes, these again more or less lobed. **Desert globemallow,** S. *ambigua,* is similar except its yellowish-green leaves are only shallowly lobed. It usually occurs at the higher altitudes in the Park. **Cheeseweed** or **common mallow,** *Malva neglecta,* is a low spreading plant of disturbed ground, bearing round, mucilaginous fruits (sometimes eaten by children) which has been introduced in the South Campground area.

ST. JOHNSWORT FAMILY, *Hypericaceae*

Common St. Johnswort, *Hypericum formosum,* with yellow petals, many stamens and oblong-ovate leaves with black dots, has been reported for the Park.

TAMARISK FAMILY, *Tamaricaceae*

One species, **Tamarisk** or **saltcedar,** *Tamarix pentandra,* a finely branched shrub with scale-like leaves and clusters of small pinkish flowers, has become widely distributed along water courses throughout southwestern North America. It was introduced by very early travellers from the Mediterranean region (see fig. VII).

VIOLET FAMILY, *Violaceae*

Garden pansies and violas belong to this group. *Viola,* the most common genus, is characterized by having an *irregular* flower; that is, it is not radially symmetrical but has 2 petals directed upwards, 2 lateral petals, and 1 directed downwards. **Wanderer violet,** *V. nephrophylla,* is the common purple one found on moist, shaded banks such as below Weeping Rock. It is widely distributed in the western United States.

117. **Canada violet,** *V. canadensis,* has white flowers and long-tipped, heart-shaped leaves. It occurs in cool, moist canyons.

FIGURE 116. Gooseberryleaf globemallow

TOM BLAUE

FIGURE 117. Canada violet
SCALE: 1 x 1

171

118. **Charleston Mountain violet,** *V. charlestonensis,* has yellow flowers and roundish leaves which often have a purplish tinge. It is rare but may sometimes be found along the upper part of the West Rim Trail and might be found in other places on the plateaus. The name comes from the Charleston Mountains in eastern Nevada where the plant was first found.

BLAZING-STAR FAMILY, *Loasaceae*

These plants have rough foliage which makes them stick to clothing or fur. On this account they are often called "stickleaf." Blazing-star is another name. Some have yellow, star-shaped flowers which open towards evening.

119. **Desert blazing-star,** *Mentzelia pumila,* with bright yellow petals and shining white stems, grows in the Lower Sonoran Zone. *M. Multiflora,* which is similar, has been seen near Rockville. **Whitestem stickleaf,** *M. albicaulis,* has small day-blooming yellow flowers and occurs on the East Zion Plateau.

FIGURE 118. Charleston Mountain violet

RUTH NELSON

172

FIGURE 119. Desert blazingstar

FIGURE 120. Claret cup

CACTUS FAMILY, *Cactaceae*

Cacti are some of the most interesting plants in the Park. Their large, conspicuous, brilliantly colored flowers can usually be seen in May. They belong to the group called "succulents," desert plants which have the ability to store water in fleshy stems or leaves for use during dry periods. In the case of cacti it is the stems which become reservoirs. These have a green bark which performs the function of leaves, manufacturing plant food, sugars and starches, by the process of *photosynthesis*. Carolyn Trapp has written an interesting booklet, *The Cacti of Zion National Park*, which is available at the Visitor Center and recommended to all who are interested in this group. In it all kinds of cacti found in the Park are described in detail. On that account only a few of the ones with particularly conspicuous flowers are described here; other names are listed. Native species fall into 3 groups: the hedgehog type, those forming mound-shaped clumps of cylindrical stems; the cholla type (pronounced choi' ya), those with branching stems made up of cylindrical joints; and the prickly-pear type, those with flattened joints. The prickly-pears are the most numerous and widely distributed in the Park.

120. **Claret cup,** *Echinocereus triglochidiatus*, is a handsome plant with scarlet blossoms, which occurs at low altitudes especially along the south edge of the Park. This is in the hedgehog group.

121. **Purple torch,** *E. engelmannii*, is even more striking and comparatively rare. Its individual stems are larger than those of the claret cup, and there are usually fewer of them.

FIGURE 121. Purple torch

174

122. **Engelmann prickly-pear,** *Opuntia phaeacantha,* or *O. engel-mannii,* is a large, branching plant with pads (stem joints) 8 to 15 inches long. It has satiny petals of a soft yellow and numerous dark red pear-shaped fruits. There are some fine examples in the planters in front of the Visitor Center. The fruits of this are edible and used by Indians and others for making jelly and candy. The 2 species are difficult to distinguish and possibly not distinct.

123. **Utah beavertail,** *O. basilaris aurea,* is the most commonly seen of the prickly-pear group. It occurs on the lower canyon slopes and the lower plateaus. It has large pink or magenta blossoms. The photograph taken after a very wet season shows the pads conspicuously swollen with stored water. **Dollarjoint cactus,** *O. chlorotica,* is a rare upright prickly-pear with short trunk and round pads. **Cliff prickly-pear** or **old man,**

FIGURE 122. Engelmann prickly-pear, *fruit*

176

FIGURE 123. Utah beavertail, *pads much swollen after rainy season*

O. erinacea, with large pink flowers, is found only in the Lower Sonoran Zone. **Whipple cholla,** *O. whipplei (O. multigeniculata),* has very spiny, sausage-shaped joints. **Golden** or **silver cholla,** *O. echinocarpa,* with greenish-yellow flowers, grows only at the lowest elevations and is more common south of the Park.

OLEASTER FAMILY, *Elaeagnaceae*

124. **Roundleaf buffaloberry** or **silverbush,** *Shepherdia rotundifolia,* is the only native representative of this family. It is an evergreen shrub with roundish leaves which are usually convex and appear as though of beaten silver. The small flowers are yellow. It is common on rocky slopes throughout the Park. **Russian olive,** *Elaeagnus angustifolia,* with narrow, almost white leaves, occurs in some of the washes as an escape from cultivation.

FIGURE 124. Roundleaf buffaloberry

RUTH NELSON

178

FIGURE 124. *Leaves and flowers*

FIGURE 124. *Leaf and flower detail*

This family is characterized by having 4 petals, 8 stamens and an *inferior* ovary. In many of the species the calyx tube, called here a "flower-tube," is extended considerably beyond the ovary so that the flower appears to be on a slender stalk. But actually this apparent stalk is a tube which is part of the flower and through which the *style*, a thread-like tube, connects the potential seed bodies, *ovules*, in the ovary with the *stigma* which receives the pollen. In fertilization the sperm cells travel through this tube from the stigma to the ovules. Many species in this family have white or yellow petals, and their flowers open in late afternoon or evening, usually withering before the next noon if the sun is bright. As they wither they turn color, the white ones becoming pink and the yellow ones orange or reddish. These light flowers attract night-flying insects which pollinate them.

 I. Plants with white or yellow petals, flowers opening towards evening (except yellow day-primrose).

 A. Petals white, becoming pink when wilted.

125. White tufted evening-primrose, *Oenothera caespitosa,* has conspicuous fragrant white flowers 3 to 4 inches across on flower-tubes 2 to 3 inches long which rise from a tuft of narrow leaves. There are 8 stamens and 4 narrow lobes to the stigma. These flowers usually open after dark and are most conspicuous in early morning.

FIGURE 125. White tufted evening-primrose

126. **Pale evening-primrose,** *O. pallida,* has a branching whitish stem and similar but smaller flowers. Its buds and stems are often reddish. This is common throughout the Park on sandy soils and is one of the plants which continues blooming during the hot summer months.

B. Plants with yellow petals.

1. Blooming in the evening.

127. **Yellow tufted evening-primrose,** *O. flava,* has pale yellow petals and grows in low tufts. It occurs in a grassy meadow near Lava Point and at other places on the plateaus, beginning to bloom about dusk. *O. primiveris* is similar but has larger flowers and grows along the road south of Zion National Park. **Tall yellow evening-primrose,** *O. longissima,* has bright yellow blossoms on flower-tubes about 3 to 4 inches long. It occurs on the plateaus. The **common evening-primrose,** *O. strigosa (O. biennis),* is similar but has smaller flowers and is found along roadsides and on disturbed ground.

2. Blooming in the daytime.

FIGURE 126. Pale evening-primrose
SCALE: 1 x ¾

FIGURE 127. Yellow tufted evening-primrose

128. **Desert day-primrose,** *O. brevipes,* has leafless stems.

129. **Yellow day-primrose,** *O. multijuga,* keeps its blossoms open during the day. Its leaves, which are mostly at the base, are irregularly divided with the widest part near the tip, and have heavy, sometimes red veins on the under side. A very small, annual, yellow-flowered day-primrose is *O. contorta.* This grows in sandy soil in shaded places on the East Zion Plateau. Its flowers are about ¼ inch across and may sometimes be reddish.

II. Plants with red or pinkish flowers.

130. **Hummingbird trumpet** or **firechalice,** *Zauschneria garrettii,* has bright red flowers which appear in late summer and fall, even to late October. The scarlet flower-tube about an inch long is trumpet-shaped with a slight swelling at the base, and the 2-lobed petals are inserted near the top. A long slender style bearing the 4-lobed stigma protrudes. The foliage is grayish. Hothouse fuchsias are closely related to this. The native plant occurs in rocky places of the Upper Sonoran and Transi-

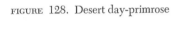
FIGURE 128. Desert day-primrose

ALLEN MALMQUIST

184

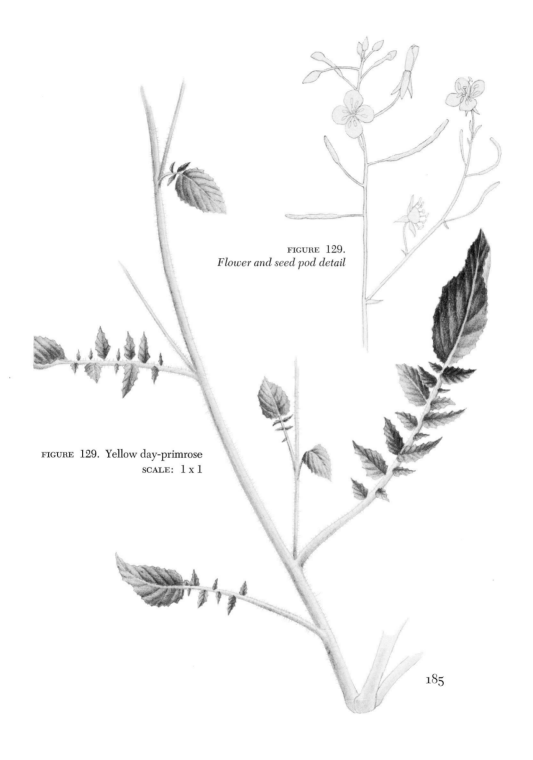

FIGURE 129.
Flower and seed pod detail

FIGURE 129. Yellow day-primrose
SCALE: 1 x 1

185

tion Zones. **Scarlet gaura** or **butterflyweed,** *Gaura coccinia,* is a branched plant with 4 to 8 inch long spikes of white or pinkish flowers less than an inch long. The petals turn reddish in aging, which gives the spikes a 2-toned appearance. This has been found only in Coalpits Wash.

III. Inconspicuous species with minute flowers.

Other members of the family in this area are: **Autumn willowherb,** *Epilobium paniculatum,* with rose or lilac flowers about an inch across and seeds bearing tufts of white hairs, which has been found at Lava Point. **Sticky willowherb,** *E. adenocaulon,* also occurs and is similar but has shreddy bark and smaller flowers. **Ground smoke,** *Gayophytum nuttallii,* a much-branched plant with slender stems and small red or pinkish flowers is sometimes found on the plateaus.

PARSLEY FAMILY,*Umbelliferae*

Plants of this family have hollow stems, compound leaves, and flowers arranged in *umbels* (see diagram in glossary, no. 23, p. 317). Flowers are white, yellow or purplish.

I. Leaf segments elongated with smooth edges.

A. Flowers white, plant small, growing on moist, shaded clay banks on the high plateaus.

131. **Indian potato,** *Orogenia linearifolia,* blooms in early spring as soon as the snow melts. It has small clusters of white flowers with maroon anthers. Most of its leaf segments are long and narrow, almost grass-like. Each stem comes from a small, roundish tuber about an inch long. These tubers furnished a starch food for the Indians. The plump seeds in tight clusters are dark at maturity.

B. Flowers yellow.

Nuttall biscuitroot or **desert parsley,** *Lomatium nuttallii,* is whisk-broom-like, 8 to 10 inches tall.

II. Leaves parsley-like.

A. Plants not over a foot tall.

186

FIGURE 131. Indian potato
SCALE: 1 x 1

FIGURE 130. Hummingbird trumpet

ALLEN MALMQUIST

187

132. **Wild parsley,** *Cymopterus purpureus,* has yellow or purplish flowers followed by clusters of purplish, winged seeds. It blooms in early spring close to the ground and occurs commonly throughout the Park on sandy soil. As the seeds develop, the stems become more or less erect. **Chimaya,** *C. fendleri,* is similar, but the leaf segments are thicker and grayish. This blooms very early in sandy areas on the East Plateau. *C. multinervatus,* with gray foliage and purplish clusters of broadly winged seeds, occurs on clay soil in the Petrified Forest area. **Nevada biscuitroot,** *Lomatium nevadense,* with gray foliage and compact umbels of white flowers, has been found in clay soil on the high ridges in the northern part of the Park.

B. Plants from 1 to 3 feet tall.

Sweet cicely, *Osmorhiza depauperata,* is about a foot tall and has compound leaves twice-divided into threes with toothed leaflets. Its seeds are club-shaped. It grows in cool, shaded locations. **Sweetroot,** *O. occidentalis,* is 2 to 3 feet tall. Its seeds are slender club-shaped with distinct beaks. It also grows in cool, wet places. *Lomatium dissectum,* a tall plant with ball-like clusters of tiny yellow flowers, grows on moist, shaded slopes near Lava Point. **Water parsnip,** *Berula erecta,* is a tall plant with pinnate leaves, the leaflets toothed or incised, and umbels of white flowers, found growing in ponds.

Other species which have been reported are: *Cymopterus bulbosus, C. newberryi, C. rosei, Lomatium orientale, L. triternatum.*

FIGURE 132. Wild parsley

FIGURE 132. *Leaf and fruit detail*

GINSENG FAMILY, *Araliaceae*

Only one species of this family occurs in the Park, and it is rare. **Wild ginseng,** *Aralia nudicaulis,* is similar to the taller members of the parsley family except that its stem is not hollow. It is known only from the Grotto and the Narrows.

DOGWOOD FAMILY, *Cornaceae*

One shrub of this family occurs in the Park. It has opposite leaves and branches.

Red-osier dogwood, *Cornus stolonifera,* grows along streams on the plateaus. It has red bark and clusters of small white flowers followed by whitish berries which are attractive to birds. Its leaves are pinnately veined and turn a deep red color in autumn.

SILK-TASSEL FAMILY, *Garryaceae*

This is a family of evergreen shrubs which have opposite leaves. Their flowers are in catkin-like clusters, the male and female on different plants. Only one species is present in Zion National Park.

133. **Silk-tassel bush,** *Garrya flavescens,* is a shrub from 4 to 10 feet tall with squarish branches and pale, leathery, hairy, short-stalked leaves about 2 inches long. It may be found along most of the trails in the canyon but is nowhere common.

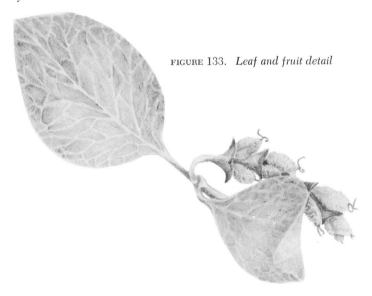

FIGURE 133. *Leaf and fruit detail*

FIGURE 133. Silk-tassel bush
SCALE: 1 x ¾

PYROLA FAMILY, *Pyrolaceae*

Only one member of this family is found in this area.

134. **Woodland pinedrops,** *Pterospera andromedea,* occurs very rarely in the ponderosa pine forests of the Kolob Plateau. It has a tall, hairy, brown stalk usually seen with brown seedpods hanging from it. In flower it has white petals. This plant is a *saprophyte,* having no green color. It is able to obtain its food from decaying wood or leaf-mold. Members of this family are closely related to those of the heath family which follows. In some books it will be found included in that family. The main difference is that in the pyrolas the petals are mostly separate, but in the heaths and those following they are united.

HEATH FAMILY, *Ericaceae*

The members of this family and those which follow differ from all the ones described before this by having their petals joined together. The term *corolla* is often used for the united petals. The corollas may be of different forms (see glossary illustrations, p. 315).

The only local representatives of this family, which includes many showy ornamental plants such as rhododendrons and azaleas, are the manzanitas of the genus *Arctostaphylos.* They are intricately branched evergreen shrubs with smooth red bark. Two species of this genus are found abundantly in Zion National Park. They are quite similar and appear to hybridize so that positive identification is difficult. They bloom in early spring with abundant small jug-shaped flowers of pink or white, which are followed by hard, green, reddish or brownish berries in summer.

FIGURE 134. *Fruiting stalk*

FIGURE 134. Woodland pinedrops

193

135. Greenleaf manzanita, *A. patula,* usually has ovate or rounded, bright green leaves. **Pointleaf manzanita,** *A. pungens,* typically has narrower, more pointed and duller green leaves. Both are found throughout the Upper Sonoran and Transition Zones.

PRIMROSE FAMILY, *Primulaceae*

The members of the true primrose family (for evening-primrose family see p. 180) have a 5-lobed united corolla and 5 stamens attached to the inside of the corolla tube, opposite to its lobes.

136. **Shooting star,** *Dodecatheon pulchellum,* is found on moist banks especially under dripping rocks. The pointed pink corolla lobes are turned back from the short tube, and the dark-colored anthers protrude, forming the tip of the "shooting" star. All its leaves are in a rosette at the base. The plant is especially abundant and lush on and below Weeping Rock and near the cliff at Emerald Pools. **Brookweed,** *Samolus floribundus,* is an inconspicuous aquatic plant with loose clusters of small white flowers occasionally found growing in ponds.

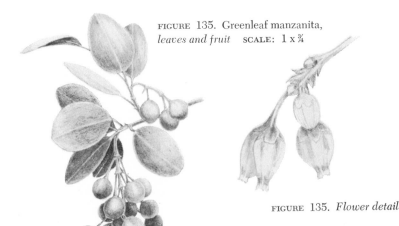

FIGURE 135. Greenleaf manzanita, *leaves and fruit* SCALE: 1 x ¾

FIGURE 135. *Flower detail*

194

FIGURE 136. *Flower detail*

FIGURE 136. Shooting star, *basal leaves*
SCALE: 1 x 1

195

OLIVE FAMILY, *Oleaceae*

The local representatives of this family are trees or shrubs with opposite branching and winged seeds. The flowers appear before the leaves.

137. **Velvet ash,** *Fraxinus velutina,* is a deciduous tree common on the floor of the canyon. Its opposite leaves have 3 to 7 lanceolate or ovate leaflets (sometimes obovate). The gray bark is broken into symmetrically checkered patterns.

138. **Singleleaf ash,** *F. anomala,* is a shrub often having several main stems which may be up to 20 feet tall but in Zion is ordinarily 4 to 8 feet. It usually has only a single leaflet but may sometimes have 3. It is common on dry rocky slopes and in dry canyons, where it is conspicuous in spring when it puts out clustered tassels of green flowers and light green leaves which turn pale yellow in autumn.

FIGURE 137. Velvet ash
SCALE: 1 x 1

196

FIGURE 138. Singleleaf ash
SCALE: 1 x 1

197

GENTIAN FAMILY, *Gentianaceae*

The flowers of this family may have almost flat or deeply cup-shaped corollas which may be either 4 or 5-lobed.

139. **Green gentian** or **elkweed**, *Frasera speciosa (Swertia radiata)*, is a tall stout plant (up to 6 feet) with pale green leaves and many 4-pointed green flowers on short stems crowded along almost the whole length of the stalk. It occurs on the high plateaus. **Whitemargin gentian**, *Frasera albomarginata*, has somewhat similar flowers, but the stalk, which may be branched, is only about 18 inches tall and the leaves have conspicuous white margins. It is a Lower Sonoran species found in Coalpits Wash. A rare, bright blue gentian is *Gentiana affinis*, which blooms in late summer in meadows on the high plateaus. **Rose gentian** or **amarella**, *G. amarella*, has been reported. **Centaury** or **"canchalagua,"** *Centaurium calycosum*, is a small pink-flowered plant with an erect stem and narrow pale green leaves which grows on moist soil and has been found along the stream in Coalpits Wash.

DOGBANE FAMILY, *Apocynaceae*

This is a family of mostly tropical plants including the cultivated oleander. Most of its members have a milky sap. Some produce rubber, and many are poisonous.

Indian hemp, *Apocynum cannabinum*, is a slender plant up to 4 feet tall with milky juice. It has opposite leaves which are lighter beneath, small white flowers, and long slender pods, sometimes in pairs. Its dry, shreddy bark was used by Indians to make a fine cord for weaving. This grows in moist locations and may be seen along the Narrows Trail.

MILKWEED FAMILY, *Asclepiadaceae*

These plants have very interestingly arranged flowers which are adapted to insure cross-pollination. The stamens and style are joined, and there are curious appendages which prevent insects from escaping without carrying pollen masses with them to the next flower visited. There are two pistils united by a common stigma which often results in a pair of seedpods. Each seed is furnished with a tuft of silky hairs which act as a parachute and so insure distribution.

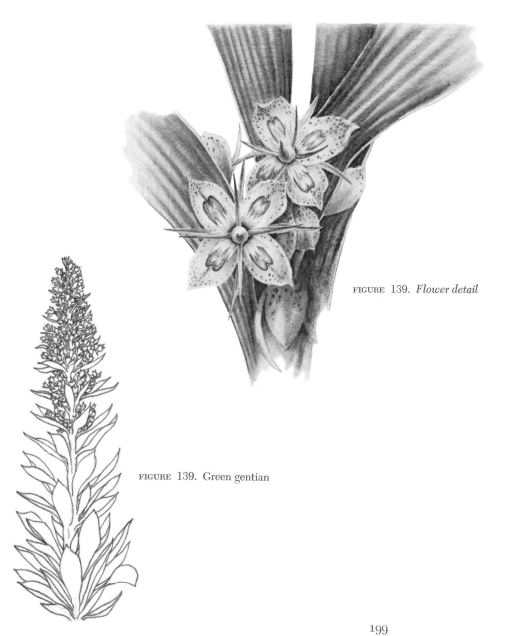

FIGURE 139. *Flower detail*

FIGURE 139. Green gentian

199

140. **Butterflyweed** or **pleurisy-root,** *Asclepias tuberosa terminalis,* is an exception in the family, not having the usual milky sap. It is very showy, usually having bright orange flowers, but they may be from yellow to orange-red. The plant is more or less hairy, and its narrow leaves are pointed.

141. **Poison milkweed,** *A. subverticillata (A. galioides),* has very narrow leaves 1 to 5 inches long, whorled on the main stem; flowers are white or greenish-purple; pods 2 to 4 inches long. **Swamp milkweed,** *A. incarnata,* has reddish flowers and grows in damp places on the plateaus. **Showy milkweed,** *A. speciosa,* has broad, ovate or oblong, thick leaves. Its stems are usually in clumps, from 18 inches to 4 feet tall. The pink or rose-colored flowers are in terminal clusters.

FIGURE 140. Butterfly weed

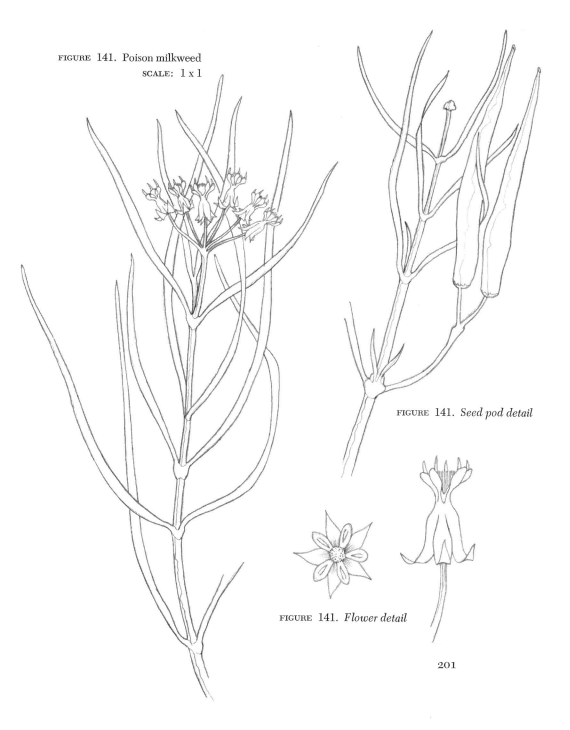

FIGURE 141. Poison milkweed
SCALE: 1 x 1

FIGURE 141. *Seed pod detail*

FIGURE 141. *Flower detail*

201

MORNING-GLORY FAMILY, *Convolvulaceae*

One weedy species of this family has been introduced and has become established along roads near the South Entrance. **Field bindweed,** *Convolvulus arvensis*, is a creeping plant with small, broadly funnel-shaped, white or pink flowers.

DODDER FAMILY, *Cuscutaceae*

Dodder, *Cuscuta cephalanthi*, is a parasite with yellow, thread-like, leafless stems which spreads in a tangled mass over other vegetation, absorbing nourishment from green plants by means of penetrating root-like structures. It has been reported from the Petrified Forest region.

PHLOX FAMILY, *Polemoniaceae*

There are many variations in this family. Corollas are always united but may be salver-form, funnel-form or nearly flat (see p. 315). They usually have 5 lobes and 5 stamens, but may occasionally have 4. Leaves are often opposite but may be alternate; they are often entire but may be lobed, dissected, or even compound. Ovaries are 3-celled and form dry capsules. Some species are handsome and conspicuous, others small and rarely noticed. Lobes of the corolla are said to be *convolute* in the bud, that is one edge overlapping the next. This is especially noticeable in the buds of phlox.

   I. Plants mat-forming, stems not erect, leaves narrow and sharp-pointed.

142. **Desert phlox,** *Phlox austromontana*, is an abundant early spring flower with white, bright pink, or lavender corollas. It forms compact or loose mats. The opposite leaves are very narrow and sharp-pointed. Its stems are only a few inches high. On dry, sunny slopes the mats are very compact; in shaded, more moist situations it has a looser form, sometimes even trailing.

FIGURE 142. Desert phlox

FIGURE 142. *Leaf and flower detail*

203

143. **Longleaf phlox,** *P. longifolia,* has similar flowers but longer stems and leaves and is much less compact. It grows among shrubs on the high plateaus. **Stansbury phlox,** *P. stansburyi,* is a hairy, more or less sticky plant with grayish leaves crowded together. It may be found in the Petrified Forest and other dry areas.

II. Plants not mat-forming, stems erect or plants bushy.

A. Flowers mainly white.

144. **Nuttall gilia,** *Linanthastrum nuttallii,* has phlox-like flowers which are white with a yellow throat. Leaves are not rigid and are so deeply divided into linear lobes that they appear whorled. **Prickly-phlox,** *Leptodactylon pungens,* has leaves with narrow divisions which are stiff and sharp-pointed, making the plant prickly. It is woody at base. Flowers are white or cream with funnel-form corollas. It often grows in rock crevices or very rocky places and is found throughout the Transition Zone.

Evening-snow, *Linanthus dichotomus,* is a slender annual plant with white or cream-colored flowers which open towards evening. A closely related and similar plant is *L. bigelovii.*

FIGURE 143. Long-leaf phlox

ALLEN MALMQUIST

FIGURE 144. Nuttall gilia

Shrubby ballhead gilia, *Gilia congesta,* is a small shrub with compact heads of white flowers. The stems and heads are more or less woolly.

B. Flowers mainly blue or lavender.

Bristly langloisia, *Langloisia setosissima,* is a small annual desert plant with woolly stems and long white bristles, mostly in pairs, on leaves and calyx. The blue corollas flare into a broad funnel-form from a very slender tube. It is found growing in Coalpits Wash. *Eriastrum wilcoxii* is somewhat similar to the last but lacks the bristles. It occurs in sandy places on the floor of Zion Canyon. *Gilia scopulorum* is a very common but inconspicuous plant. It has small, blue, or whitish or pinkish flowers and pinnately lobed leaves which are mostly in a basal rosette. It is found throughout the Park.

C. Flowers yellow or light orange.

145. **Cream-phlox,** *Collomia grandiflora,* grows in oak woods, especially below Emerald Pools and at Birch Creek. These plants are erect, 10 to 40 inches tall with pointed, lance-shaped leaves and cream-colored to salmon-yellow, narrow funnel-form corollas with spreading lobes. A small yellow-flowered gilia relative about 1 to 5 inches tall is *Navarretia breweri.* It is usually branched from the base, and its leaves are pinnately lobed with narrow, spine-tipped segments. It occurs on the high plateaus.

D. Flowers bright red.

146. **Skyrocket,** *Gilia aggregata,* is a conspicuous summer-blooming plant of the plateaus, especially in ponderosa forests. It has a salver-form corolla with slender tube usually over an inch long with 5-pointed, somewhat reflexed lobes about ¼ inch long. **Arizona skyrocket,** *G. arizonica,* is shorter and somewhat stouter, with a tube usually less than an inch long and lobes about ⅜ inch long, which occurs in the Lower Sonoran Zone, especially the Coalpits Wash and Petrified Forest areas. Two small, inconspicuous members of this family are *Gilia polycladon,* with pinnately lobed leaves at the base of a bare stem which has a leafy cluster of small white flowers; and *Microsteris gracilis* which has small white flowers and small, oblong, entire leaves, the lower ones opposite, hairy and tending to be reddish, along a stem 4 to 8 inches tall.

FIGURE 145. Cream-phlox

FIGURE 146. Skyrocket

Most plants of this family have their flowers arranged in coiled clusters, some have the stamens protruding from the corolla so that the anthers are conspicuous, some have pinnately lobed leaves and others have entire, or almost entire leaves. All have the seeds contained in capsules.

I. Plant a woody shrub with narrow, sticky leaves.

Yerbasanta or **mountain balm,** *Eriodictyon angustifolium,* is a shrub found on dry hillsides at low altitudes in the Park and outside along the west boundary. Its leaves are sticky, fragrant, narrow and white underneath. It has clusters of white or pale lilac flowers with bristly sepals and protruding stamens. A tea made from the leaves was used by the pioneers as a remedy for colds and sore throat.

II. Plants not woody.

Phacelia, *Phacelia.* All the species in the Park except the **varileaf phacelia,** are annual. Leaves vary from being pinnately, finely divided to undivided. Flowers are white, pale lavender, sky blue or purple.

147. **Fremont phacelia,** *P. fremontii,* has a sky blue corolla ½ inch across with yellow throat, and pinnately lobed leaves, the small lobes with round ends. Most of the leaves are basal. This is one of the most beautiful flowers in the Park, but it is conspicuous only in seasons of plentiful rainfall. It grows in the shade of shrubs in desert areas such as the Petrified Forest and along the lower Watchman Trail.

148. **Varileaf phacelia** or **caterpillar plant,** *P. heterophylla,* is one of the very common plants of Zion National Park. It is a perennial with rough, hairy foliage and coarsely lobed, grayish leaves. Its flowers are in conspicuously coiled clusters, pale lavender with prominently protruding stamens. It occurs on dry or moist hillsides, along trails, and often on disturbed soil.

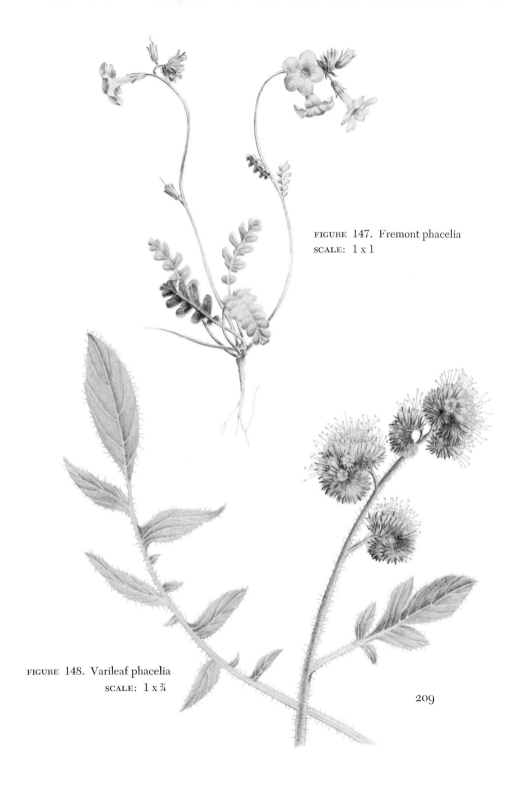

FIGURE 147. Fremont phacelia
SCALE: 1 x 1

FIGURE 148. Varileaf phacelia
SCALE: 1 x ¾

209

149. **Purple scorpionweed** or **wild heliotrope**, *P. crenulata*, with sticky and strong-smelling foliage and purple flowers with protruding stamens, is very common on dry gravelly fields and slopes through much of southern Utah and Arizona. In Zion it occurs only at the lowest altitudes, particularly at Coalpits Wash. *P. affinis* is a small, inconspicuous plant with pale purple flowers not over ⅓ inch long. It grows in sandy areas, often under the shade of shrubs.

P. pulchella is a very small plant with round, oblong or ovate, wavy-edged leaves and rather conspicuous purple, yellow-throated corollas. It occurs in the Lower Sonoran Zone. *P. curvipes* has blue to violet, bell-shaped corollas with white throats, about ¼ inch long, and oblong to long-obovate leaves ½ to 1 inch long. Usually these leaves have smooth edges, but they may sometimes have one or more short lobes. This is found on dry sandy areas of the Upper Sonoran and Transition Zones. **Death Valley phacelia**, *P. vallis-mortae*, has been reported for the Park.

Hesperochiron pumilus is a small low plant with all its smooth-edged leaves in a basal rosette. White or pale lilac flowers are borne singly on slender stalks 1 to 2 inches long. The inside of the corolla is hairy. This grows on rich, moist soil near Potato Hollow and probably in other similar situations on the plateaus. *Tricardia watsonii* is an interesting plant of desert regions which has been found at Coalpits Wash. It has very small purple and white flowers. After blooming 3 of the sepals enlarge, forming a heart-shaped fruit ½ to 1 inch long.

150. **Squaw-lettuce** or **western waterleaf**, *Hydrophyllum occidentale*, has rounded clusters of lavender flowers from which the stamens and styles protrude giving a fringed effect. The flower stalks are only

FIGURE 149. Purple scorpionweed

210

slightly, if any, taller than the long pinnately divided leaves which are mostly basal. It grows on moist ground in the shade of trees in the side canyons.

BORAGE FAMILY, *Boraginaceae*

Many of the plants of this family have their flowers in *scorpioid* (coiled) clusters. At first these may be so tight as to seem like heads, but as the flowers mature, the stalk begins to uncoil. Those in the Park have regular, 5-lobed corollas which are salver-form or funnel-form. Most of these plants are rough-hairy, sometimes even bristly. The ovary is 4-celled and at maturity separates into 4 *nutlets* with distinctive characteristics. They may be smooth and shiny, winged, or prickly. Several garden favorites, especially forget-me-nots, and some troublesome weeds, such as stickseeds, are in this family.

I. Flowers, or inflorescences, conspicuous.

    A. Flowers yellow, white, or yellow and white, corolla salver- or trumpet-shaped; day blooming.

        1. Foliage with all the hairs appressed to the leaf surface.

151. Puccoon, *Lithospermum incisum,* has clusters of beautiful clear yellow, trumpet-shaped flowers. The earliest ones which come in April are over an inch long and nearly an inch broad. Later in the season the flowers are much smaller. The narrow leaves are hairy. It grows on stony slopes and benches in the Upper Sonoran and Transition Zones. **Manyflower puccoon,** *L. multiflorum,* is similar and grows in similar places but has smaller, orange-yellow flowers.

        2. Foliage usually bristly and individual flowers small.

Cryptantha, *Cryptantha.* These are usually bristly plants; their corollas, white or yellow, resemble the flowers of forget-me-nots in form. They have narrow, blunt leaves. Their nutlets may be smooth and shiny or more or less roughened but never prickly. The genus divides into two groups: the first consists of perennial plants with conspicuous inflorescences; the second, described under section II (p. 216), consists of annuals with very small flowers.

FIGURE 150. Squaw-lettuce
SCALE: 1 x ¾

FIGURE 151. Puccoon

RUTH NELSON

213

Ballhead cryptantha or **yellow forget-me-not**, *C. confertiflora*, has yellow flowers at first crowded into a head 1 to 2 inches across and with a few smaller clusters along the stem lower down. This often has several stems up to 20 inches tall and is the most common of the showy species in the Park; it is found in the Upper Sonoran Zone.

152. **James cryptantha**, *C. jamesii*, has white flowers and usually several stems less than 10 inches tall from a woody crown. *C. jamesii pustulosa* has similar flowers but is taller.

153. **Yelloweye cryptantha**, *C. flavoculata*, has the corolla lobes white or cream-color and the throat yellow. It usually grows at higher altitudes than the last one. **Virgin River cryptantha**, *C. virginensis*, is a very bristly plant, the bristles turning yellowish as the plant ages, with small, white flowers and usually several stems up to 15 inches tall. It is a desert species and has been found in Coalpits Wash.

B. Flowers blue, corolla tubular-bell-shaped.

FIGURE 152. James cryptantha
SCALE: 1 x ¾

214

FIGURE 153. Yelloweye cryptanth

ALLEN MALMQUIST

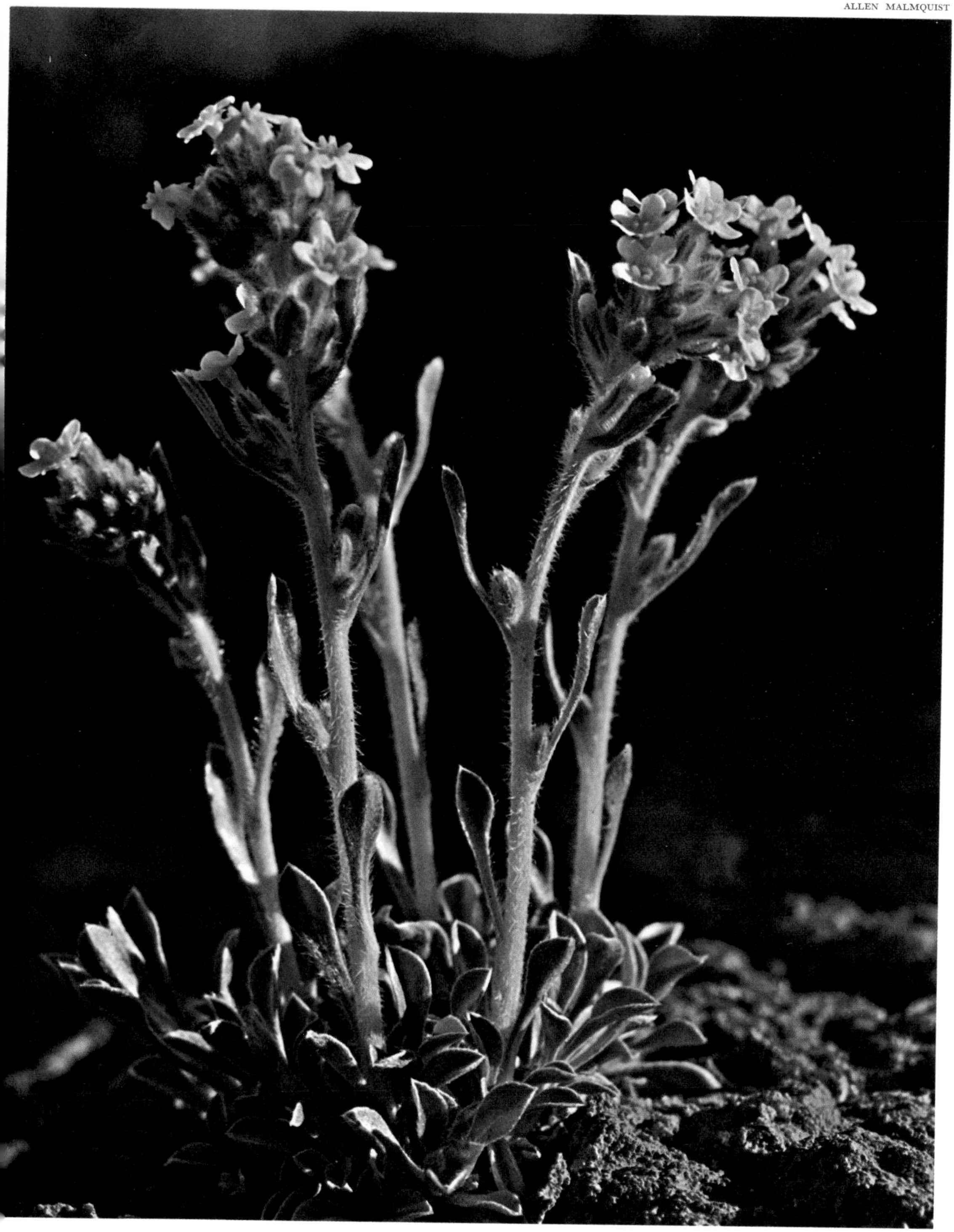

Bluebells, *Mertensia*. These are leafy-stemmed plants a foot or more tall having clusters of hanging blue flowers. They grow in woods on the plateaus. **Arizona bluebells**, *M. arizonica*, has blue corollas about ½ inch long and smooth ovate or lance-shaped, pointed leaves up to 4 inches long.

154. **Spindleroot bluebells** or **Utah mertensia**, *M. fusiformis*, has smaller flowers and more or less blunt leaves which have appressed hairs on their upper surfaces which all point toward the nearest edge.

C. Flowers white, about ½ inch broad, blooming in evening.

Heliotrope, *Heliotropium convolvulaceum californicum*, has white fragrant flowers which open in late afternoon. The plant is rough-hairy with yellowish-white hairs from enlarged bases. It occurs in sandy places.

II. Flowers inconspicuous, white, yellow or pale blue.

A. Nutlets without prickles, plants erect. Foliage usually bristly.

Several annual species of **cryptantha** fall into this group. Cryptanthas have their nutlets without prickles though they may be roughened. This distinguishes them from similar plants of other related genera. **Slender cryptantha**, *C. gracilis*, is a loosely spreading plant 4 to 10 inches tall with slender branches which are appressed hairy but not bristly. Its tiny white flowers are in rather loose clusters outlined by soft white bristles. *C. pterocarya* is similar but taller and more erect. Its nutlets are wing-margined. Another similar erect but bristly species is *C. decipiens*. A bristly small plant 4 to 16 inches tall with erect stem and basal rosette of ovate leaves is *C. watsonii*. It occurs in moist, sandy areas. Two **fiddlenecks**, *Amsinkia menziesii* and *A. retrorsa*, are other bristly plants with fiddleneck-like flower clusters which have been reported from the East Entrance area. Their flowers are yellow.

B. Nutlets with prickles making them bur-like, but foliage not strongly bristly.

Tall stickseed or **false forget-me-not**, *Hackelia floribunda*, has light blue forget-me-not-like flowers in an elongated cluster and bur-like seeds. The plant may be up to 4 feet tall. *H. patens* is similar but not so tall and with a more open inflorescence. Its flowers may be white or

216

FIGURE 154. Spindleroot bluebells
SCALE: 1 x 1

217

pale blue. Both grow on the plateaus. **Common stickseed,** *Lappula redowskii,* is an annual, branching plant of disturbed ground with white or bluish flowers and many "sticktight" seeds. **Combseed,** *Pectocarya setosa,* is a small annual plant of desert areas having its 3 or 4 bristly nutlets arranged in 2 opposite pairs. The flower stalks become bent down in fruit.

VERBENA FAMILY, *Verbenaceae*

The only local representative of this family is **bigbract verbena,** *Verbena bracteata,* a low-spreading plant with irregularly pinnately lobed leaves and spikes of small blue or purplish flowers. It is found around buildings or along roads.

MINT FAMILY, *Labiatae or Lamiaceae*

This family is similar to the borage family in having its fruits composed of 4 nutlets, but differs from it and is easily recognized because of the square stem, opposite leaves and irregular corolla which is usually 2-lipped. Most of the species are aromatic. It includes several garden herbs such as mint, sage, lavender, thyme and others. Its flowers are good sources of nectar for honey.

I. Plants woody.

155. **Desert sage,** *Salvia dorrii carnosa,* is a handsome small shrub when in bloom. The clustered flowers are brilliant blue and surrounded by broad, purplish bracts. It occurs at lowest altitudes in the Park and especially on slopes back of and west of the Visitor Center.

II. Plants not woody except, in some cases, at the base.

A. Plants tall, sometimes to 4 feet.

Common motherwort, *Leonurus cardiaca,* grows on disturbed ground on the high plateaus around pastures. Its opposite leaves are palmately 3 to 5 parted, hairy and lighter colored beneath; flowers are in dense axillary clusters with pink or white corollas less than ½ inch long; the upper lip is woolly with hairs.

FIGURE 155. Desert sage

FIGURE 155. *Flower detail*

156. **Giant hyssop**, *Agastache urticifolia*, is another tall plant of the plateaus. It has green, long-triangular, coarsely-toothed leaves and compact terminal spikes of small pinkish flowers.

B. Plants not over 2 feet tall and more or less widely branched.

Mock pennyroyal, *Hedeoma nanum*, is a gray plant, 4 to 8 inches tall and much-branched from the base. The leaves are gradually reduced upwards, the lowest not over ½ inch long; the flowers are light purple, each with a white spot and purple lines. It occurs on dry rocky slopes. **Monardella**, *Monardella odoratissima*, is 6 to 14 inches tall from a more or less woody base. Its leaves are green and covered with fine, short hairs. Flowers are pale purple with exserted stamens, calyx woolly around the short teeth. The plant is very fragrant.

Molucca-balm, **shell-flower**, or **bells of Ireland**, *Moluccella laevis*, is an annual, smooth, light green plant. Its flowers are in whorls of 6 with a 3-spined bract below each cluster. Individual flowers are inconspicuous, but the calyxes are flaring green bells each an inch or more broad. This plant, which escaped from cultivation, occurs near Petrified Forest. **Field mint**, *Mentha arvensis*, is more or less hairy, has its flowers in whorls in the leaf axils, and has opposite lance-shaped to oblong or ovate, toothed leaves. These plants have spreading underground stems so they often occur in patches. They have a strong mint odor. **Spearmint**, *Mentha spicata*, has its flowers in terminal spikes. It is naturalized from Europe and occurs around dwellings.

Some other introduced members of this family occur on disturbed soil around settlements and along trails: **Horehound**, *Marrubium vulgare*, is commonly seen about the Visitor Center. Its stems are covered with a thick mat of white woolly hairs. **Catnip**, *Nepeta cataria*, has been found along the Weeping Rock Trail. Its pointed, toothed leaves are green and more or less hairy. **Dragonhead**, *Moldavica parviflora*, has its flowers in dense, oblong spikes interspersed with spine-tipped bracts. **Wild-basil**, *Clinopodium vulgare*, has been reported as growing in the Park.

FIGURE 156. Giant hyssop
SCALE: 1 x ¾

221

FIGURE 157. Tomatilla

POTATO FAMILY, *Solanaceae*

The flowers of this family have regular, 5-lobed, wheel-shaped or funnel-form corollas. Fruits are 2-celled berries which are either smooth, enclosed in a husk, or prickly. Some species are important vegetables such as potatoes, tomatoes, peppers and eggplants; others are important ornamental garden plants such as petunias. Still others are very poisonous.

157. **Tomatilla** or **wolfberry**, *Lycium pallidum*, is a stout, spiny, crookedly branched shrub having sessile, pale green, obovate leaves and narrow, funnel-form, greenish-white or purplish flowers from ½ to nearly 1 inch in length. Its juicy red berries are ¼ to ⅜ inch in diameter.

FIGURE 157. *Leaf and flower detail*

222

158. **Anderson wolfberry,** *L. andersonii,* has smaller leaves and flowers, and blooms and fruits earlier than the tomatilla. Both are Lower Sonoran desert shrubs and occur in Zion at the lowest altitudes, as at the Watchman Trailhead. The berries of both were a staple article of food for the Indians. **Wild tobacco,** *Nicotiana trigonophylla* and *N. attenuata* are coarse, sticky herbs with tubular whitish flowers which may be found in the Petrified Forest area.

159. **Sacred datura** or **jimson weed,** *Datura metaloides,* is the most showy of the group. It is a large coarse plant with white or lavender funnel-form corollas 6 to 8 inches long which open in the evenings and are conspicuous in the early mornings. The fruits are large prickly berries. The plants are poisonous with narcotic qualities and were used by some Indian tribes in religious ceremonies.

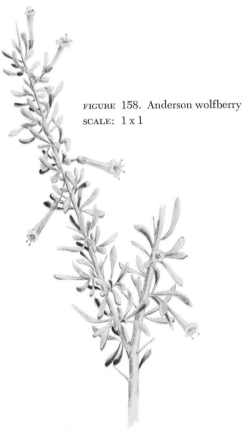

FIGURE 158. Anderson wolfberry
SCALE: 1 x 1

FIGURE 159. *Fruit detail*

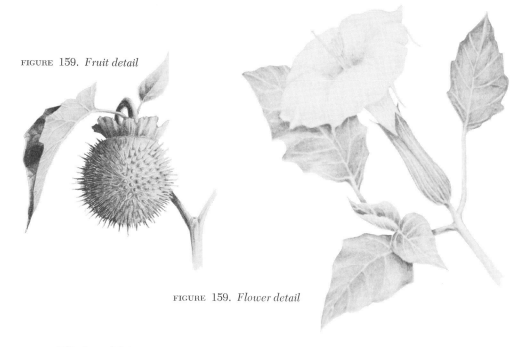

FIGURE 159. *Flower detail*

FIGURE 159. Sacred datura

160. **Fendler groundcherry** or **husk tomato,** *Physalis fendleri,* has an open bell-shaped corolla, yellow with a brown center. The thin leaves are more or less triangular with wavy edges and have very small hairs on the under surface, some of which are 2-forked. (It takes a 10x lens to see these.) In fruit the calyx enlarges, becoming an inch or more long, and encloses the berry. These berries were eaten by the Indians. *P. hederaefolia* is similar, but its foliage is sticky and lacks the 2-forked hairs. Both grow on dry rocky banks. **Black nightshade,** *Solanum nigrum* (or *S. nodiflorum*), has smooth, triangular, wavy-edged leaves, white flowers and black berries which are said to be poisonous. **Cutleaf night-shade,** *S. triflorum,* is more or less hairy, has pinnately lobed leaves and green berries. Both are widely distributed but not common.

FIGWORT or SNAPDRAGON FAMILY, *Scrophulariaceae*

This is a large and varying family with many showy wild flowers and several cultivated varieties such as snapdragons and foxgloves. The united corollas are mostly irregular, usually 2-lipped. The leaves may be alternate or opposite, usually not divided but may be more or less lobed or toothed.

I. Leaves pale, densely woolly.

Mullein, *Verbascum thapsus,* is a tall, stout biennial plant. The first year it forms a handsome rosette of thick woolly, oval or obovate leaves 6 to 12 inches long which persist through the winter. The second year a tall stalk grows up with gradually smaller leaves and a dense spike of yellow flowers. This plant was naturalized long ago from Eurasia and occurs on dry banks and disturbed ground.

II. Leaves various but never densely woolly.

A. Leaves alternate or mainly basal.

Paintbrush, *Castilleja.* In this genus the flowers, which have incon-spicuous corollas, are crowded into terminal spikes; calyxes are brightly colored and flowers are interspersed with brightly colored bracts, thus forming the "brush."

161. **Early Indian paintbrush,** *C. chromosa,* is one of the earliest plants to bloom in Zion. In late March you may see the first brilliant

226

FIGURE 160. Fendler groundcherry
SCALE: 1 x ½

FIGURE 161. Early Indian paintbrush

red "brushes" on dry slopes near Oak Creek or near the Watchman Trailhead. Later they will be conspicuous along the Scenic Drive and up the Mount Carmel Road. The plant is usually in clumps of several stems and is commonly found in sagebrush areas or in the pinyon-juniper pygmy forest. Leaves are narrow and may be entire or have 1 or 2 pairs of narrow lobes. The red-tipped bracts usually have 2 pairs of short lobes.

162. **Slickrock paintbrush,** *C. scabrida,* has leaves with narrow, pinnate lobes. Its flowers are brilliant orange-scarlet with narrowly lobed bracts. This grows in tufts in crevices of the slickrock. *C. miniata* is another similar red-flowered species found on the plateaus.

163. **Wyoming paintbrush,** *C. linariaefolia,* is a branching plant up to 2½ feet tall with scarlet calyxes and bracts. The corollas are usually green with a narrow red edge to the upper lip, about 1½ inches long and protruding from the calyx. Leaves are narrow, sometimes pinnate with narrow lobes. This is widely distributed at all altitudes in the Park.

FIGURE 162. Slickrock paintbrush

228

FIGURE 163. Wyoming paintbrush
SCALE: 1 x 1

FIGURE 162. *Flower detail*

229

Wood betony, *Pedicularis centrantha,* is a woodland plant found on the plateaus where it forms small carpets. It has a basal rosette of white-edged, pinnately divided leaves and short stalks bearing few flowers. The flowers, 1 to 1½ inches long, are purplish or yellowish, sometimes 2-toned, with a hood-shaped upper lip. **Birdbeak,** *Cordylanthus parviflorus,* is a much-branched plant, dingy-looking because it is covered with short, sticky hairs. Its rose-purple, finely hairy flowers are scattered along the branches. It grows on dry rocky slopes. **Wright birdbeak,** *C. wrightii,* which has clustered, brownish-pink or yellowish flowers, has been found on the East Rim. **Owlclover,** *Orthocarpus luteus,* is a slender annual plant, often unbranched, with a thick dense spike of yellow flowers. The lower lip of the irregular corolla is sac-like. Individual flowers are separated by protruding, green, 3 to 5-lobed bracts. This has been reported from Zion Canyon.

B. Leaves opposite.

Monkey flower, *Mimulus.* This genus contains several very showy species and some very small-flowered inconspicuous ones. The calyx is usually angular and has 5 lobes that are pointed. In some species the upper lobe is noticeably longer than the other lobes. The corollas are mostly strongly 2-lipped; often the opening is nearly closed by 2 ridges on the lower lip. The corollas of yellow-flowered species are often spotted with red, and the calyxes are often spotted.

164. **Scarlet monkey flower,** *M. cardinalis,* is a lush plant of wet banks and stream sides. The brilliant corollas are about 2 inches long, bright orange-scarlet with a yellow throat. Leaves are in pairs, the upper without stalks and clasping the stem. This is frequently seen on and below Weeping Rock, along the Narrows and at Emerald Pools. Since it grows only in cool places where there is a perpetual supply of water, it may be found in bloom at almost any time in the summer.

Yellow monkey flower, *M. guttatus,* with bright yellow corollas and spotted calyx, is smaller and grows in the same sorts of places and also along streams on the plateaus. Its flowering season is limited to early summer. *M. nasutus (M. guttatus depauperatus)* is a similar but smaller yellow-flowered species. **Parry monkey flower,** *M. parryi,* is a low an-

230

FIGURE 164. Scarlet monkeyflower

nual desert plant with corollas up to an inch long which are usually purple but may be yellow. This has been found at the Cinder Cone and in Coalpits Wash. Some small annual species occurring in the Park are: *M. rubellus*, with either yellow or pink flowers; *M. floribundus*, a yellowish, hairy and sticky plant with small yellow flowers; and *M. suksdorfii*, a low, reddish, compactly-branched plant ½ to 2½ inches tall with yellow funnel-form corollas. It is found only occasionally and grows in moist, sandy places on the plateaus.

165. **Blue-eyed Mary,** *Collinsia parviflora,* is a small branched plant with blue and white irregular flowers in the axils of upper leaves or bracts. The leaves and stems are often reddish. It is widely distributed in shady places on the plateaus. **Speedwell** or **brooklime,** *Veronica americana*, is a trailing plant of wet ground with small blue flowers sometimes found around springs on the plateaus.

Penstemon, *Penstemon.* This is a large group of plants with many species growing naturally in the west and southwest states. Corollas are united, irregular, and in most cases 2-lipped, with the upper lip of 2 lobes, the lower of 3. There are 5 stamens (*pen* meaning 5 and *stemon* meaning stamen) which are attached to the inside of the corolla, but only 4 are functional. The fifth has no anther and is often tufted with yellow or orange hairs. This character accounts for the common name, **beard tongue,** for this group. Not all species in the Park have bearded "tongues." The leaves are both opposite and basal.

C. Lower leaves continuous around the stem.

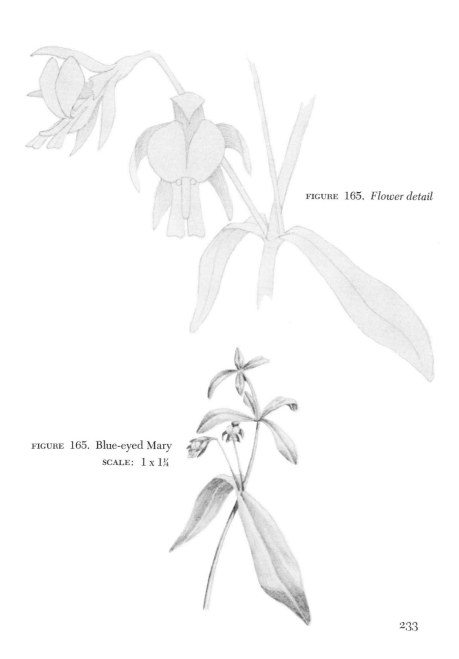

FIGURE 165. *Flower detail*

FIGURE 165. Blue-eyed Mary

SCALE: 1 x 1¼

233

166. **Palmer penstemon,** *P. palmeri,* is one of the most conspicuous and handsome plants of the Park. It usually has several or many stems 2 to 3 feet tall. Its leaves are thick and grayish, the lower ones joined around the stem, the upper leaves reduced in size and often pointed. The fat, pink or whitish corollas are an inch long and nearly an inch across and delicately fragrant. These plants are abundant on the slopes about Zion Canyon, blooming in late May and June.

    D. None of the leaves continuous around the stem, but they may clasp the stem.

      1. Corollas definitely bright red.

FIGURE 166. *Flower detail*

234

FIGURE 166. Palmer penstemon, *plants may be up to four feet tall*

167. **Utah penstemon,** *P. utahensis,* is the earliest one to bloom and a most beautiful plant. Corollas are a rich carmen or crimson with a velvety texture and spreading, rounded lobes. Leaves are light bluish-green, several in a basal rosette and smaller, narrower ones oppositely arranged along the stems. It is abundant on the slopes and along trails, beginning to bloom in early April.

FIGURE 167. Utah penstemon

RUTH NELSON

FIGURE 167. *Flower detail*

168. **Eaton penstemon** or **firecracker penstemon**, *P. eatonii*, has scarlet or orange-red flowers with narrow funnel-form corollas, the lobes not spreading but the light yellow anthers slightly protruding. Leaves are a dark green. The basal ones have long stalks, and the stem leaves are sessile, varying in shape from obovate to almost heart-shaped. It may begin to bloom as early as late April and is frequently seen in May and early June throughout the canyons and on the plateaus. **Scarlet bugler** or **Torrey penstemon**, *P. barbatus torreyi*, is somewhat similar, but its corolla is more deeply lobed and the 3 lower lobes are turned back. It has been found on the plateaus in the Park but is rare. **Bridges penstemon**, *P. bridgesii*, is a bushy plant somewhat woody at base with stems from 1 to 3 feet tall. Its scarlet, tubular corollas are finely sticky both inside and out. It grows on the plateaus, often in rock crevices.

2. Corollas not red.

A. Corollas about an inch long.

169. **Royal penstemon**, *P. laevis*, has a bright purple-blue, 2-lipped corolla which expands abruptly from a short tube into a rounded throat. Stems are in erect clumps, 8 inches to 3 feet tall. Basal leaves are

FIGURE 168. Eaton penstemon
SCALE: 1 x 1

238

FIGURE 169. Royal penstemon

lanceolate to spatulate, 1 to 3 inches long on slender petioles; narrow and sessile stem leaves are gradually reduced in size upwards. This species is variable as to color, size and habit. It occurs throughout the Park. Another species, *P. leiophyllus,* is similar and difficult to distinguish. **Dusty penstemon,** *P. comarrhenus,* has large light blue flowers. Its anthers are covered with woolly hairs.

       B. Corollas usually less than 1 inch long.

Thickleaf penstemon, *P. pachyphyllus,* (*pachyphyllus* means thickleaf) has numerous blue-purple flowers set close to the main stalk. Leaves are bluish with blunt, rounded ends. It tends to grow in patches and is found from the Lower Sonoran Zone to the Transition Zone.

170. **Low penstemon,** *P. humilis,* is a slender plant rarely more than a foot tall. The corolla, about ½ inch long, is blue with a white throat. The inflorescence is finely hairy and sticky. Most of the leaves are sharp-pointed, but in the subspecies *P. humilis* ssp. *obtusifolius,* found on the plateaus, the basal ones are apt to be blunt. **Siler penstemon,** *P. linearioides sileri,* is a low-growing plant, not over 8 inches tall, with crowded, linear leaves and one-sided, erect clusters of small, purple-blue flowers. This plant often forms mats under ponderosa pines on the high plateaus.

Leonard penstemon, *P. leonardii,* 8 to 10 inches tall, has purple flowers about ½ inch long with the sterile stamen not bearded. It grows from a woody crown, and its stems are woody at the base. **Gilia penstemon,** *P. ambiguus,* a bushy plant of sandy regions which has pink buds but corollas with white faces, is said to grow near the South Entrance.

FIGURE 170. Low penstemon

SCALE: 1 x 1¼

DEVILSCLAW FAMILY, *Martyniaceae*

171. **Devilsclaw** or **unicorn-plant,** *Proboscidea parviflora,* is the only member of this family in the Park. It is a spreading plant which often grows in a mat form. The snapdragon-like flowers are reddish or white with red spots. The interesting fruits lose their fleshy outer coat leaving a woody pod with a long curved tip which splits, resulting in 2 horns; the whole pod may be 6 to 9 inches long. This occurs at Coalpits Wash near the Park's southern boundary and possibly elsewhere in the Lower Sonoran Zone.

BROOMRAPE FAMILY, *Orobanchaceae*

This is a family whose members are parasitic on the roots of other plants. They lack all green coloring substance so are dependent on obtaining their food from other living plants. Their flowers resemble those of the snapdragon family. Two species of **broomrape,** *Orobanche,* are found in the Park.

FIGURE 171. Devilsclaw, *ripened and dried seed pod*
SCALE: 1 x 1

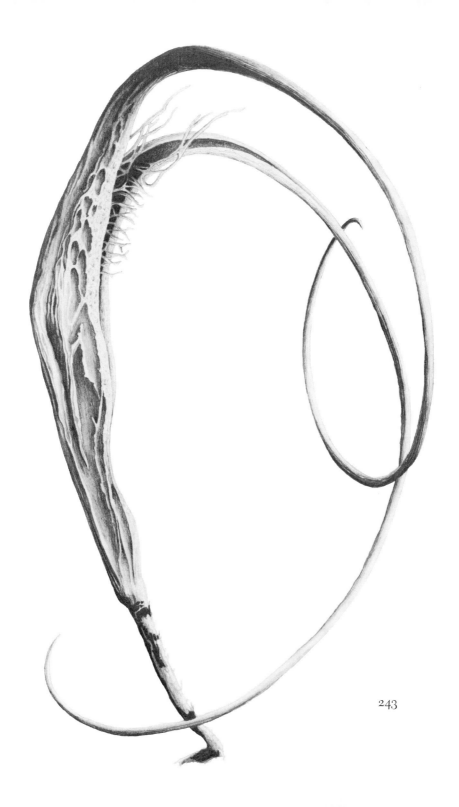

243

172. *O. ludoviciana* is a brownish, sticky, hairy plant with a thick stem and several pinkish-brown flowers on erect stalks. The picture shows a yellow form, var. *lutea*. *O. fasiculata* is rather purplish with many purple flowers on short stalks, forming a dense, elongated cluster.

PLANTAIN FAMILY, *Plantaginaceae*

The plants of this family are inconspicuous. The commonest species is **Pursh plaintain,** *Plantago purshii,* a low silvery annual with very narrow leaves from 1 to 4 inches long covered with long silvery hairs. The small 4-parted corollas are papery. **Common plaintain,** *P. major,* is a non-native plant with broad-ribbed green leaves sometimes found in lawns or other moist places.

MADDER FAMILY, *Rubiaceae*

Members of this family may be recognized by their 4-angled stems, opposite or whorled leaves, and tiny white or yellowish flowers with 4-lobed corollas. The fruits are 2-lobed, often covered with short hooked hairs.

173. **Catchweed bedstraw** or **cleavers,** *Galium aparine,* is an annual with 6 narrow leaves at a node and fruits nearly ¼ inch across when mature, covered with hooked bristles.

FIGURE 173. Catchweed

SCALE: 1 x ¾

FIGURE 172. Broomrape, *the yellow form*

JEROME GIFFORD

174. **Shrubby bedstraw,** G. *multiflorum,* is a small bushy plant often seen on dry banks and along trails. Its stems and ovate leaves are rough. Leaves are usually less than ½ inch long and are arranged in 4's. Its small white corollas are 4-lobed, and the 2-lobed fruit is densely covered with short bristles. **Twinleaf bedstraw,** G. *bifolium,* is a soft annual plant having 2 (or sometimes 4) oval or oblong leaves at each joint. It is smooth except for the fruits and is rarely over 6 inches tall. It grows in moist, shaded places. G. *proliferum* is similar but more slender and has 4 leaves at each joint. G. *asperrimum* is a very rough perennial plant with, usually, 5 or 6 leaves at each joint. **Madder,** *Rubia tinctorum,* is a coarse rough plant similar to the bedstraws but much larger with yellow flowers. It is a dye plant which was brought in by the early settlers and has become naturalized.

HONEYSUCKLE FAMILY, *Caprifioliaceae*

Species of this family are either shrubs or woody, trailing plants. Their leaves are always opposite, and the flowers have united corollas and *inferior* ovaries, that is, the corolla is attached to the top of the ovary.

Snowberry or **buckbrush,** *Symphoricarpos.* These plants are shrubs with pink tubular or funnel-form corollas, white berries and shreddy bark.

175. **Parish snowberry,** S. *parishii,* is a low, glaucous-leaved shrub. Its flowers, about ½ inch long, hang from the leaf axils, often in pairs. Its leaves are finely hairy. Its grows in Hidden Canyon, along the West Rim Trail and in other moist, cool situations. **Longflower snowberry,** S. *longiflorus,* has dainty pink salver-form corollas in the upper leaf axils, and its neat, bluish, very finely hairy leaves are about ½ inch long. It occurs on dry slopes around Zion Canyon. **Mountain snowberry,** S. *oreophilus,* has smooth twigs and leaves and grows on the high plateaus. **Utah snowberry,** S. *oreophilus utahensis,* is similar but has its young twigs pubescent and its flowers about ½ inch long. S. *vaccinoides,* with trailing stems, is found in cool, moist situations as along the Hidden Canyon Trail.

246

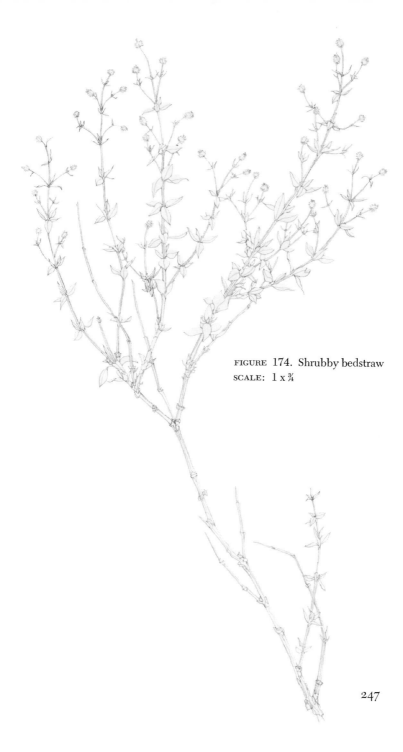

FIGURE 174. Shrubby bedstraw
SCALE: 1 x ¾

247

Elderberry, *Sambucus caerulea,* is a stout shrub usually having several stems. It may be from 2 to 15 feet tall and has large, compound leaves of 5 to 9 saw-edged leaflets. The small white flowers are in flattish clusters and are succeeded by numerous small bluish berries. This grows in moist canyons of the plateaus.

VALERIAN FAMILY, *Valerianaceae*

Western valerian, *Valeriana occidentalis,* is the only representative of this family in the Park. It has a basal rosette of smooth leaves with stalks and a stem about a foot tall with clusters of small white flowers. It grows in moist places.

GOURD FAMILY, *Cucurbitaceae*

This is the family to which all the squashes, pumpkins, melons and cucumbers belong.

176. **Wild gourd** or **calabazilla,** *Cucurbita foetidissima,* occurs on the floor of Zion Canyon. It is a trailing plant with large, gray, triangular

FIGURE 175. Parish snowberry
SCALE: 1 x ¾

248

FIGURE 176. Wild gourd
SCALE: 1 x ½

leaves with tendrils opposite them and yellow bell-shaped flowers about 4 inches long. The green and white gourds are about the size of baseballs.

BELLFLOWER FAMILY, *Campanulaceae*

177. **Cardinal flower** or **western lobelia**, *Lobelia cardinalis graminea*, is the most showy red flower found blooming in Zion National Park from mid-August to October. Stalks are 1 to 3 feet tall and carry spikes of dense, rich red blossoms. The corolla is 2-lipped with 2 small lobes above and 3 below. It occurs on moist banks and in other wet locations.

COMPOSITE or SUNFLOWER FAMILY, *Compositae*

Don't be afraid of the composites! If you read the following paragraphs and observe the drawings on p. 318, you will be able to identify many of them.

These plants are called composites because their inflorescence is made up of small individual flowers closely packed together in a specialized arrangement called a *head*. This head appears to be a single flower, but if you take a dandelion or a sunflower head and break it apart you can easily see the separate flowers. These flowers are very highly developed in the evolutionary sense and streamlined to carry on the function of the reproduction of the species. In a ripening sunflower head, or a dandelion going to seed, you can observe the parts of the individual flower (see p. 318). They are always arranged on a supporting structure called the *receptacle*. The ovary is *inferior*, and when fertilization has taken place a small fruit called an *achene* develops. The corolla is united, the calyx has become modified into something called the *pappus*, or in some cases is absent. The pappus may be of many hair-like bristles or of few or many flattened bristles or scales arranged around the base of the corolla. It is usually white or light brown and is often very conspicuous as the heads go to seed. It acts as a parachute, as seeds are carried by the wind which insures wide distribution.

The stamens and pistil, inside the corolla, in many species become functional at different times; at one stage the stigmas may be raised above the corollas; at another the anthers may protrude. This helps to

FIGURE 177. Cardinal flower, *blooms in autumn*

insure cross-pollination. There are three main types of heads in this family. Most conspicuous are those with *radiate* heads like the asters and sunflowers. In this type there are two kinds of flowers in each head, the *disk* flowers which have more or less symmetrical, tubular corollas and the *ray* flowers in which the corollas, though tubular at base, become split and flattened or strap-shaped. The flowers with these strap-shaped corollas surround the cluster of disk flowers and, collectively, are called the *ray*. In a sense they correspond to "petals." The second group has heads composed only of flowers with tubular corollas like the disk flowers; and the third only of ray-like flowers, of which the dandelion is an example.

In all members of this family there is a protective structure which appears to correspond to a "calyx" and encircles the entire head. It is called an *involucre* and is made up of small scales or leaflike bracts. These are called *phyllaries* or, in some books, *involucral bracts*. They have definite forms and arrangements which help in identification (see p. 319). They may be symmetrically overlapping, as shingles on a roof, or they may be in one or more series variously arranged.

Composites make up one of the largest plant families. Many species have very small flowers and are difficult for the amateur to identify, but many have individual flowers large enough so that their details may be easily seen, especially with a 10x hand lens.

    I. Shrubs having inconspicuous flowers.

178. **Emory baccharis** or **waterwillow**, *Baccharis emoryi*, is a shrub which may be from 3 to 12 feet tall. It grows along streams and on flood plains. The male and female flower heads, which are on different plants, are in loose clusters at the upper ends of the stems. The female flowers have soft white pappus hairs about ½ inch long which make these heads more conspicuous than the male flower heads. Leaves are long, green and narrow. This shrub is commonly seen along the floor of the main canyon. An herbaceous species, *B. glutinosa*, has been reported. **Arrow-weed**, *Pluchea sericea*, has very silvery leaves and straight erect stems. It grows on wet flood plain areas as in Coalpits Wash.

FIGURE 178. *Pistillate, flower detail*

FIGURE 178. Emory baccharis, *pistillate above, staminate below*
SCALE: 1 x ¾

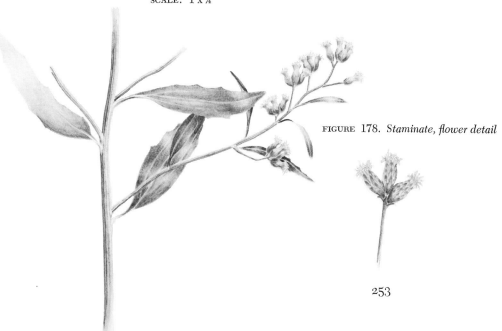

FIGURE 178. *Staminate, flower detail*

Sagebrush, *Artemisia*. There are several kinds of woody sagebrushes. They are silvery shrubs with rigid black trunks and persistent leaves. Their flower heads are small, yellowish when in bloom, and arranged along erect stems. **Basin sagebrush,** *A. tridentata,* may be up to 5 or 6 feet tall, but in Zion it is usually not over 4 feet. It has wedge-shaped, 3-toothed, silvery leaves and a strong aromatic odor. It occurs throughout the Park above the Lower Sonoran Zone.

179. **Sand sagebrush** or **old man,** *A. filifolia,* is usually 2 or 3 feet tall and has very narrow, almost thread-like, silvery leaves. It occurs in the Upper Sonoran Zone, especially in sandy places. *A. arbuscula nova,* a smaller shrub of rocky places, and *A. cana,* which usually has entire (i.e. not toothed or lobed) leaves, are also found in the Park. Other kinds of *Artemisia* which are herbs rather than shrubs occur here also. Most of them have gray leaves, but **tarragon,** *A. dracunculus,* which is used as a seasoning herb, is one that has narrow green leaves. *A. ludoviciana, A. ludoviciana mexicana* and *A. campestris scouleriana* are others found here.

White burrobrush, *Hymenoclea salsola,* is a low much-branched shrub with almost thread-like leaves from ½ to 1¼ inches long. It has two kinds of flower heads, male and female, both on the same plant. They are very small, but the female fruits have several thin, silvery, spreading, wing-like scales which make them noticeable. This is a plant of salty or alkaline soil occasionally found in the desert washes. *H. fasciculata* is similar, but the wings are smaller so it is less conspicuous.

II. Herbs with showy flowers. (Some of these plants especially **narrowleaf goldenweed,** may have their stems somewhat woody at the base.)

A. Heads all radiate, i.e. with both ray and disk flowers.

1. Heads entirely yellow.

A. Heads more than 1 inch wide (except in **three-ribbed goldenweed**).

FIGURE 179. Sand sagebrush

180. **Desert marigold,** *Baileya multiradiata,* is one of the most beautiful wildflowers in the Park. Its foliage is silvery, and its daisy-like heads, 1 to 2 inches across, are a soft clear yellow with both ray and disk the same color. The irregularly pinnately lobed leaves are at the base and on the lower part of the several stems, which may be 10 to 25 inches tall. *B. pleniradiata* is very similar, but its stems are more leafy. Both occur on the dry rocky slopes and ridges of Zion Canyon in the Upper and Lower Sonoran Zones, blooming in late May and June.

FIGURE 180. *Leaf detail*

FIGURE 180. *Flower detail*

FIGURE 180. Desert marigold   SCALE: 1 x ½

181. **Goldenaster,** *Chrysopsis villosa hispida,* is a very common, widely distributed and variable plant. Both ray and disk flowers are yellow, and the leaves are covered with rough grayish hairs. The plant is usually low, and its clustered stems, which spread outwards from the base, are 8 to 15 inches tall. It occurs along roads and trails and on dry hillsides throughout the Park.

Arnica, *Arnica latifolia,* has 2 to 4 pairs of nearly heart-shaped or ovate stem leaves and often some long-stalked, heart-shaped basal leaves. There are usually 2 or 3 heads on each stem and 8 to 12 ray flowers from ⅔ to about 1 inch long. This is found in moist places of the upper side canyons and on the plateaus.

182. **Heartleaf arnica,** *A. cordifolia,* is very similar but usually has only one head to each stem and should be found on the plateaus.

FIGURE 181. Goldenaster
SCALE: 1 x 1

FIGURE 182. Arnica

258

183. **Arrowleaf balsamroot,** *Balsamorhiza saggitata,* is a coarse plant with arrowhead-shaped basal leaves which are velvety white, especially beneath. They may become green above. The yellow flower heads are 2 to 3 inches across. It grows on the high plateaus. **Arizona mulesears,** *Wyethia arizonica,* is another coarse plant. The hairy oblong or elliptical green leaves, 8 to 15 inches long, are mostly basal with a few smaller ones on the stalks. The yellow heads are 3 to 4 inches across on stalks 12 to 20 inches tall. It is found along streams or in moist meadows on the plateaus.

Little sunflower, *Helianthella quinquenervis,* is an erect plant 2 to 4 feet tall which grows in moist woods on the plateaus. It has pale yellow rays and somewhat darker disk flowers. The heads, usually solitary, are 3 to 6 inches broad and *nodding,* i.e. at right angles to the stalk. There are about 4 pairs of stem leaves, and each leaf has 5 ribs. In the Rocky Mountains this is called **aspen sunflower.** (See also **Parry gaillardia,** p. 270).

Bush encelia, *Encelia frutescens virginensis,* is a low shrub with whitish stems and yellow, radiate heads held on stalks above the very rough leaves. It is found on rocky slopes in the Lower Sonoran Zone.

Cooper hymenoxys, *Hymenoxys cooperi canescens,* is a tall, usually grayish plant, often with only one stalk. There is a cluster of narrow, pinnately parted leaves in a rosette at the base and several which gradually became smaller up the stem. The lower basal leaves have often dried and become brown by flowering time. The yellow radiate heads are arranged in a *corymbose* (see p. 317) cluster, each head from ½ to 1½ inches broad. This occurs on slopes in dry rocky places, especially in the Petrified Forest region. *H. scaposa,* with single flower heads on 3 to 6 inch stalks, also occurs in the Park.

Goldenweed, *Haplopappus.* Plants of this group are variable. Most have ray flowers but some only disk flowers. The species in this area have yellow flowers. **Iron plant,** *H. gracilis,* is a low annual with radiate, yellow, aster-like heads similar to those of **goldenaster,** (p. 258). The edges of its leaves are set with long white bristles. This is a plant of dry ground, often found along roadsides.

260

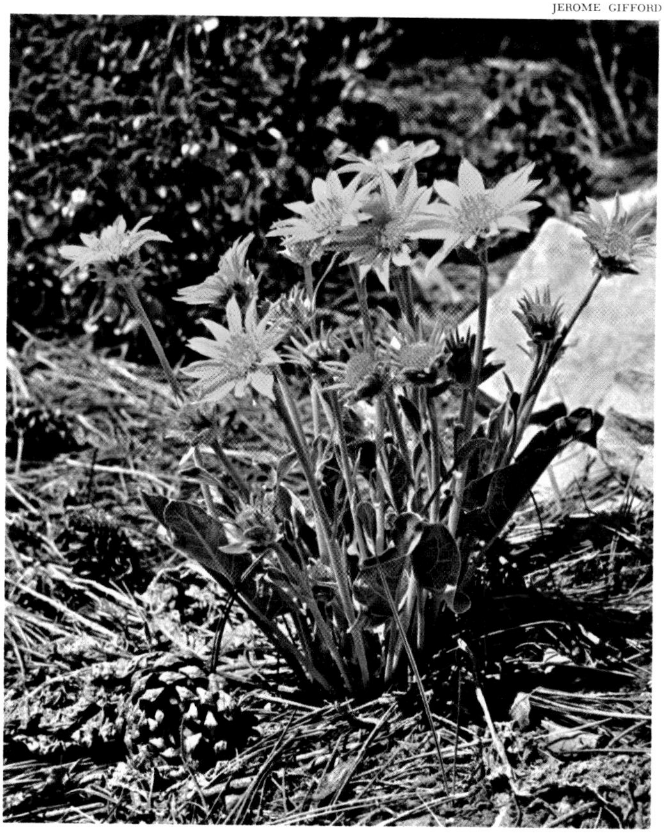

FIGURE 183. Balsamroot

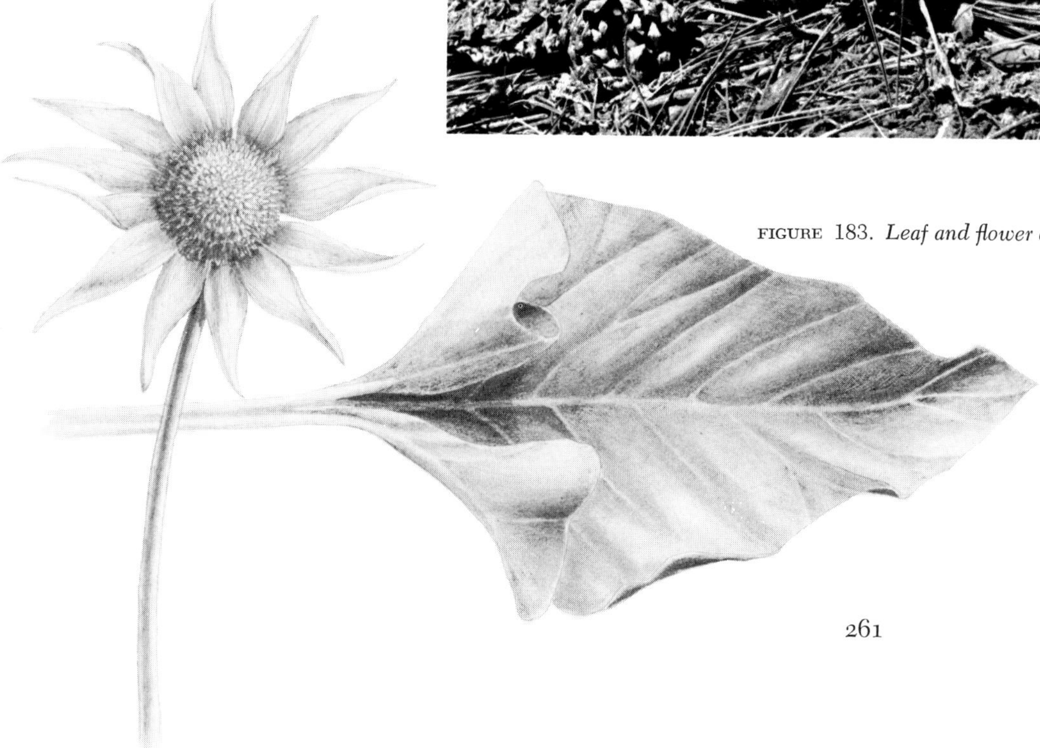

FIGURE 183. *Leaf and flower detail*

Narrowleaf goldenweed, *H. linearifolius interior,* is a low, rounded, shrubby plant with conspicuous yellow-rayed flower heads. Under a hand lens one can see that the leaves are covered with small dark dots which exude a sticky substance. This plant grows on dry rocky slopes at low altitudes in the Park. **Desert goldenweed,** *H. macronema,* which has only disk flowers and has white-felted stems, also occurs in the Park. **Three-ribbed goldenweed,** *H. scopulorum,* is a plant having several straw-colored stems about 20 inches tall with long-pointed, three-ribbed leaves. There are no ray flowers, but the disks are yellow. The phyllaries, which have green centers and papery margins, are overlapped in 6 or 7 rows. This plant resembles goldenrod, but the overlapping phyllaries and lack of ray flowers distinguish it. It grows on rocky slopes, particularly along the Watchman Trail.

Senecio or **groundsel,** *Senecio.* There are 4 different kinds of senecio (pronounced sen e′ ci o) in the Park, but they are comparatively easy to recognize and distinguish. They all have bright white pappus (tufts of hairs on each achene) which is conspicuous as the plants go to seed. The name comes from the Latin *senex,* meaning old man, because of the white hair-like pappus.

184. **Lobeleaf senecio,** S. *multilobatus,* is the one most commonly seen blooming in spring and early summer in many areas. Its stems are from 6 to 15 inches tall, often several to one plant. The stems and leaves are usually covered thinly with grayish cobweb-like hairs. The clustered heads are bright yellow, each about ½ to 1 inch across with about 13 phyllaries. Leaves may be up to 4 inches long, pinnately lobed with irregular, rounded segments. S. *streptanthifolius,* which is similar to the **lobeleaf senecio,** has been found on the East Zion Plateau along the Canyon Overlook Trail.

FIGURE 184. Lobeleaf senecio

SCALE: 1 x 1

263

185. **Lambstongue senecio,** S. *integerrimus,* is an early spring flower on the high plateaus. Its leaves have mostly smooth edges, but there may be some very small teeth. Stems and foliage are often slightly woolly especially on the young parts. The tips of the phyllaries are black, and the central head of the cluster, which blooms first, is on a stout stalk shorter than the others. S. *millelobatus* is very similar, but its heads have about 21 phyllaries, and it grows in sandy areas of the Lower Sonoran Zone.

186. **Broom senecio** or **broom groundsel,** S. *spartioides,* is one of the dominant plants blooming in late summer. It has several much-branched stems 1 or 2 feet tall forming a rounded, bushy plant. Leaves

FIGURE 185. Lambstongue senecio
SCALE: 1 x ½

264

FIGURE 186. *Leaf and flower detail*

RUTH NELSON

FIGURE 186. Broom senecio

265

are 1 to 4 inches long, very narrow, and sometimes have a few narrow lobes. Its numerous bright yellow heads are about an inch wide, the disks a darker color than the ray. This is one of the very colorful plants along roads and trails from late summer into October.

B. Heads less than 1 inch wide.

Goldenrod, *Solidago.* There are at least 4 kinds of goldenrod in Zion National Park. They are not easy to distinguish. They all have small ray flowers. **Western goldenrod,** S. *occidentalis,* is perhaps the most distinctive one. Its flower heads are in more or less roundish clusters, not one-sided or recurved. Its stems may be from 2 to 8 feet tall, but in the Park are usually 3 to 4 feet. Leaves are long-pointed, up to 4 inches long and about ¼ inch wide. The plant somewhat resembles the **three-ribbed goldenweed,** but its stem is green, not straw-colored, and the heads do have small rays. **Missouri goldenrod,** S. *missouriensis,* is another tall plant. Its leaves are shorter and wider than those of **western goldenrod.** Its flower heads are arranged in one-sided, recurving sprays, several of them branching from the main stem.

187. **Few-flowered goldenrod.** S. *sparsiflora,* is one of the commonest. **Low goldenrod.** S. *decumbens nana,* occurs on the plateaus. **Rock-goldenrod,** *Petradoria pumila,* is a flat-topped plant with numerous stems 3 to 12 inches tall bearing small clusters of small yellow heads. Most of the narrow leaves, 1 to 5 inches long, are clustered at the base of the stems. The flower heads usually have only 1 to 3 ray flowers and 3 to 5 disk flowers.

266

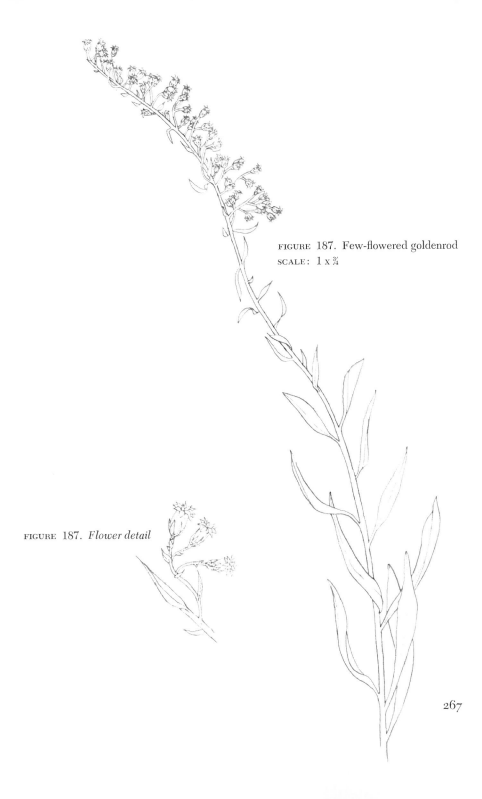

FIGURE 187. Few-flowered goldenrod
SCALE: 1 x ¾

FIGURE 187. *Flower detail*

267

188. **Broomweed,** *Gutierrezia sarothrae,* is a low bushy plant. Its stems are woody at base with narrow leaves and clusters of very small flower heads. Each head usually has from 3 to 8 small ray flowers and about the same number of disk flowers. The plant is not hairy but is slightly sticky. *G. microcephala* is very similar, but its heads are even smaller, usually having only 1 or 2 ray flowers. The inflorescences, or flower clusters, are flat-topped. This characteristic, plus the very small leaves, separate these plants from the goldenrods. Other common names for the broomweeds are **snakeweed** and **matchweed.** Both are widely distributed on dry slopes and plains throughout the Park. They often have many fine, dead twigs intermingled with the living ones.

> 2. Heads with rays yellow but disks dark colored, either brownish or dark red (except **Parry gaillardia**).

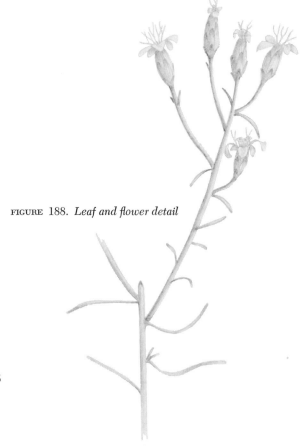

FIGURE 188. *Leaf and flower detail*

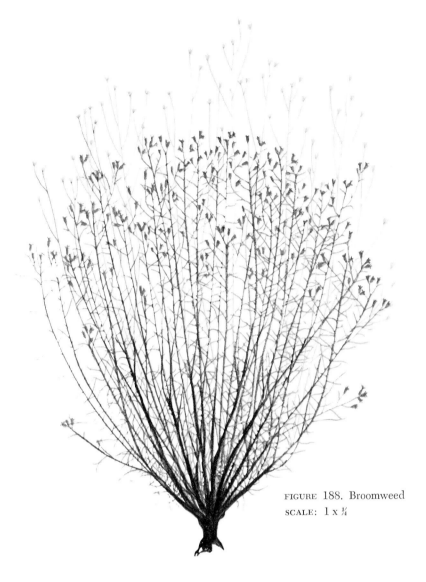

FIGURE 188. Broomweed
SCALE: 1 x ¼

269

189. **Gaillardia,** *Gaillardia pinnatifida,* has showy heads 2 to 3 inches broad with orange-yellow, wedge-shaped, toothed rays and dark red or maroon disks. Its hairy leaves are about 2 to 3 inches long and usually wavy or lobed. The plant is frequently seen on dry sandy or rocky slopes and flats of the main canyon, blooming in May and June. **Parry gaillardia,** *G. parryi,* which has entirely yellow heads, has been found near the East Entrance. Some of the gaillardias around Park Headquarters seem to be hybrids between *G. pinnatifida* and a cultivated form of *G. aristata.*

Sunflower, *Helianthus.* These are annual plants but develop rapidly and may start blooming in early summer. Two species are present in the Park: *H. annua,* the **common sunflower,** and the similar *H. petiolaris,* which is smaller and less common. Both have heads from 2 to 4 inches broad and dark disks. They usually occur on roadsides and other disturbed ground.

Showy goldeneye, *Viguiera multiflora,* is a branched plant with slender stems and flower heads about 1½ inches broad, usually with dark disk flowers. They look a little like small sunflowers. Two other species may sometimes have dark disk flowers: *Encelia frutescens* and *Helianthella quinquenervis.* For descriptions of these see p. 260.

      3. Heads with ray flowers purple, bluish or white, disks yellow.

Aster, *Aster.* These plants have radiate heads usually about 1 to 1½ inches wide. The ray flowers may be bluish, pale lavender, or white, but the disks are always yellow though they may turn burnt orange or dark reddish as they age. The pappus, of hair-like bristles, is white or light tan. Usually the phyllaries are mostly green and overlapping in 2 or 3 rows and do not have loose, recurved tips. (See p. 319.) These plants usually bloom in September and October.

Siskiyou aster, *A. hesperius,* is a branching plant from 1 to 3 feet tall with numerous purplish heads. It grows on moist soil in semi-shaded locations.

270

FIGURE 189. Gaillardia

190. **White-flowered Siskiyou aster,** A. *hesperius laetevirens*, with pale lavender, pinkish or nearly white rays, is a close relative of the one above and a similar plant except for the whitish rays. It occurs commonly on wet banks below dripping rocks and at stream sides.

191. **Glaucous aster,** A. *glaucodes pulcher*, usually has stems about 1 to 2 feet tall with many glaucous, i.e. pale bluish-green, leaves and light purple flowers. It often forms masses of pale foliage along roads and trails. **Pacific aster,** A. *chilensis (A. adscendens)*, is usually less than 2 feet tall and has only a few light purple or bluish heads. It is widely distributed in western North America but is found in Zion only at the higher altitudes.

FIGURE 190. White-flowered Siskiyou aster

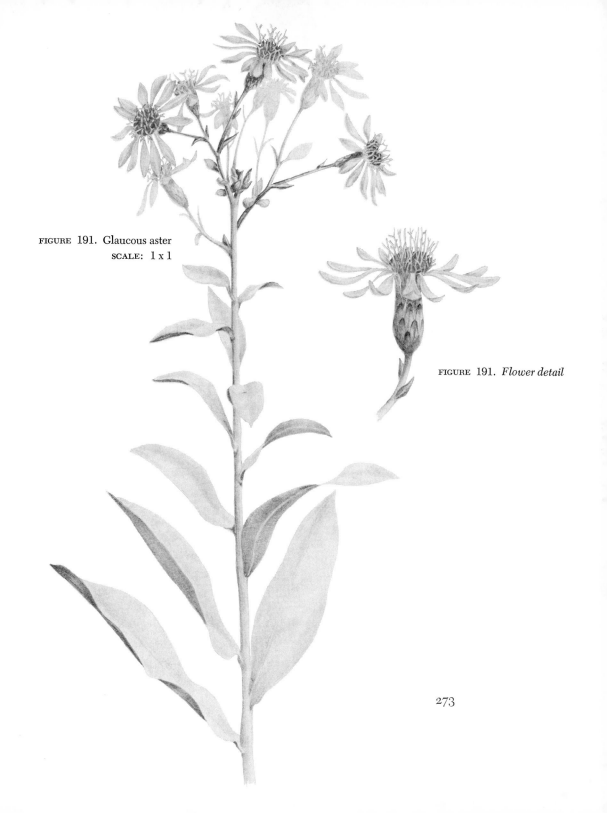

FIGURE 191. Glaucous aster
SCALE: 1 x 1

FIGURE 191. *Flower detail*

273

Tansy-aster, *Machaeranthera.* These plants are closely related but differ from the true asters in being widely branched and in having their phyllaries, which are in several series, pale with dark green recurved tips. The color of their ray flowers is a beautiful brilliant purple. The plants are conspicuous along roads and trails and on dry hillsides throughout the Park in autumn.

192. **Tansy-aster,** *M. linearis,* is the most common and contributes much of the beautiful purple color in the autumn landscape. Its flower heads are about 1 inch broad, and its leaves are narrow and irregularly toothed. *M. tanacetifolia* is similar but has somewhat larger flower heads, and the lower leaves especially are finely pinnately lobed with the lobes toothed.

FIGURE 192. *Leaf and flower detail*

274

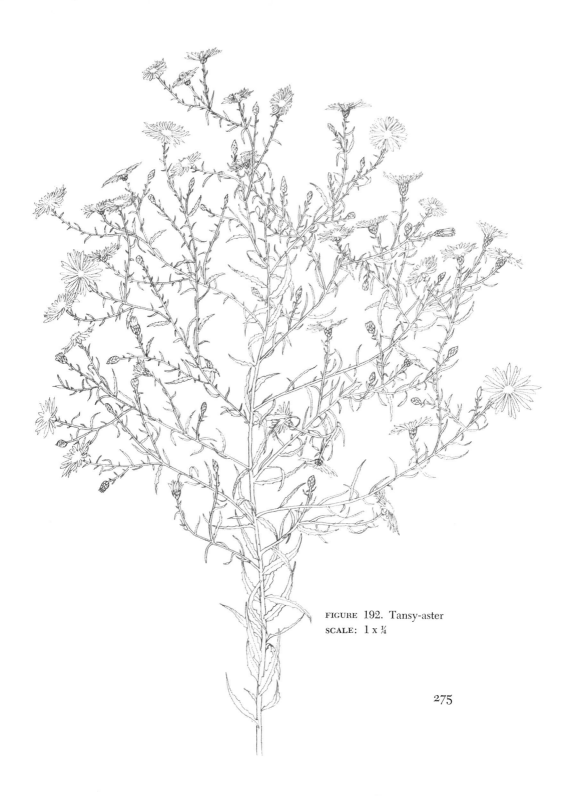

FIGURE 192. Tansy-aster
SCALE: 1 x ¼

275

Daisy or **fleabane,** *Erigeron.* The heads of these plants resemble those of the asters. They have lavender, purplish or white ray flowers and yellow disks. The two groups are sometimes difficult to distinguish. But, in general, daisies have narrower and more numerous ray flowers and disks that are wider in proportion to the length of the rays than are those of the asters. Also they are usually spring-blooming plants. The genus may be roughly divided into 2 groups. One group includes those species with comparatively few heads or, if many, then each head on a rather long individual stalk. The second group comprises those with branching stems and many heads.

Group 1. Flower heads few, or, if many, then each head on a rather long individual stalk.

193. **Utah daisy,** *E. utahensis,* is about 1 foot high, branched from the base with narrow leaves and few or sometimes many heads, each on a rather long stalk. The ray flowers are bright bluish-purple or white. It occurs on dry rocky hillsides throughout the Park and blooms in May and June.

194. **Eaton daisy,** *E. eatonii,* which grows on the plateaus, is a low, white-flowered species with many narrow, hairy leaves. **Whiplash daisy,** *E. flagillaris,* is a low plant with small heads on long slender stalks. The rays are white when the flower is open but often pink in the bud. This plant sends out runners which root at their tips and start new plants. It is common in sandy areas in spring and early summer. **Early white daisy,** *E. pumilus concinnoides,* usually grows in a clump with stems less than a foot tall. The stems and leaves are conspicuously hairy, the rays white. This occurs on dry plains and in the ponderosa forest on the plateaus.

Zion daisy, *E. sionis,* is an interesting, small, rare plant found on the faces of shaded, moist cliffs and known only from Zion National Park. It has small white flower heads and pinnately lobed leaves. There are very small narrow leaves on the stems.

Group 2. Species with much-branched stems and numerous heads.

276

ALLEN MALMQUIST

FIGURE 194. Eaton daisy

FIGURE 193. Utah daisy
SCALE: 1 x 1

277

E. religiosus is another rare plant which so far has been found only in Zion. It grows from a taproot and has small white-rayed heads on slender branched stems 2 to 10 inches tall. The oblanceolate or spatulate basal and lower stem leaves are blunt and taper to a slender stalk. It grows in sandy areas of dry, open forest on the plateaus. **Branching daisy**, *E. divergens*, is common; usually has lavender heads and grows in dry places. **Horseweed**, *Conyza canadensis*, is a plant much-branched in the upper part with many small heads which have short, inconspicuous rays.

195. **Hoary townsendia**, *Townsendia incana*, is a low plant with white or pinkish heads on short stalks set among clusters of narrow grayish leaves. It grows in sandy locations on the East Zion Plateau, at Petrified Forest, and probably in other locations, blooming in April and sometimes also in the fall. **Whitedaisy tidytips**, *Layia glandulosa*, is a branching plant from a few inches to a foot tall with hairy leaves and bright white flower heads with yellow centers. The ray flowers are 3-toothed at their tips. This grows on dry sandy areas at all altitudes in the Park. **Yarrow**, *Achillea millefolium lanulosa*, is a plant of dry open areas, especially disturbed ground, with numerous small white heads on stems 1 to 2 feet tall arranged in a corymbose (p. 317) inflorescence. The round, white rays are only about ⅛ inch wide. The disk flowers are also white. The plant has long, narrow, aromatic leaves divided into fine segments giving a fern-like appearance.

    B. Heads with flowers all alike, all with tubular corollas, no rays present.

        1. Plants with stout spines on margins of leaves and tips of phyllaries; heads more than 1 inch high.

Thistle, *Cirsium*. These are tall plants recognized by the stout spines on their usually pinnately lobed or wavy-margined leaves and on the tips of the phyllaries.

196. **Arizona thistle**, *C. arizonicum*, is a stout plant 2 to 4 feet tall with grayish foliage and beautiful red flower heads about 2 inches long. The color is distinctive for a thistle, and the heads are more or less cylindrical.

278

FIGURE 195. Hoary townsendia
SCALE: 1 x 1

FIGURE 196. Arizona thistle

197. Utah thistle, *C. utahense,* is up to 4 or 5 feet tall with round white heads on long leafless stalks. It is frequently seen on the floor and lower slopes of Zion Canyon, especially along the Scenic Drive. The central, still unopened flowers are pinkish. Other kinds of thistles found in the park are: *C. foliosum, C. pulchellum, C. undulatum* and *C. tracyi.*

  2. Plants without stout spines; some may have weak prickles; heads less than 1 inch high.

  A. Shrubs, or at least bushy in habit and more or less woody at base, with cream, bright yellow or white flowers.

Rabbitbrush, *Chrysothamnus.* The plants of this genus are shrubs from 1 to 5 feet tall. They have many erect branches from a heavy, often crooked, woody trunk. The bright yellow heads are small and massed in dense sprays crowded together on the upper part of the bush.

198. Big rabbitbrush, *C. nauseosus,* occurs in 2 forms around rocks and along roadsides on the floor of Zion Canyon and also on the lower

FIGURE 197. Utah thistle, *leaf and flower detail*

280

FIGURE 198. *Branch and flower detail*

FIGURE 198. Big rabbitbrush

plateaus: *C. nauseosus albicaulis* has whitish or gray leaves and stems and flower heads from ½ to ¾ inch high. *C. nauseosus glabratus* has green stems and leaves but is otherwise similar to the above. **Parry rabbitbrush,** *C. parryi nevadensis,* is similar but smaller and is occasionally found on the plateaus. *C. viscidiflorus stenophyllus* is a rounded shrub with white bark, usually not over 3 feet tall. Its narrow, sticky leaves are often twisted. It grows in the Upper Sonoran Zone.

199. **Longspine horsebrush,** *Tetradymia axillaris,* is a spiny shrub, 3 to 6 feet high with bright yellow flower heads. The stems and usually the spines also are covered with a felty mat of fine cottony hairs. Its principal leaves have become modified into the stiff spines which are about 1 inch long. There are clusters of small green leaves at the axils. The 5 or 6 narrow, blunt phyllaries, nearly ½ inch long, may or may not be woolly. There are 6 or 7 yellow flowers about ½ inch long with bright white pappus in each involucre. This grows on sandy desert areas of the Lower Sonoran Zone. **Gray horsebrush,** *T. canescens inermis,* has no spines, but its leaves and stems are wooly. It has yellow flowers and silky-shiny, pale tan pappus. This is a low shrub of the dry plateau regions. **Goldenhead,** *Acamptopappus sphaerocephalus,* is a twiggy shrub 1 to 3 feet tall, with small grayish leaves and rounded yellow heads less than ½ inch high. The heads are usually solitary at the ends of clustered, short, leafless stalks. This is a desert shrub which often appears half dead because of the many dead twigs extending above the living part of the plant. **Palmer laphamia,** *Laphamia palmeri,* is a bushy little plant with a woody base which grows from crevices of sandstone rock. It has ovate, sharply toothed leaves rarely over an inch long, and many light yellow, rayless flower heads. The pappus consists of 1 long bristle.

FIGURE 199. Longspine horsebrush

200. **Thoroughwort,** *Eupatorium herbaceum,* is a plant of rocky places often found growing in crevices. It has clustered small white flower heads without rays and rough, pale green, triangular or heart-shaped, toothed leaves. The leaves are mostly in pairs. The flowers turn brownish as they age. It grows on canyon slopes above 5,000 feet.

Brickellbush or **Coleo,** *Brickellia.* This group includes both shrubby plants and herbs. They resemble the thoroughworts. Their phyllaries are thin, almost papery, with strong green ribs. There are no rays, and the flowers are greenish-white or cream-color. The genus has sometimes been called *Coleosanthus.* The Zion species have whitish stems except the **large-flowered brickellbush. California brickellbush,** *B. californica,* has triangular or ovate, toothed, pointed leaves and whitish stems. The heads are about ½ inch long, and the narrow phyllaries are pale green and shiny. **Large-flowered brickellbush** or **tasselflower brickellbush,** *B. grandiflora,* has green stems, similar but somewhat larger heads and ovate or lanceolate leaves. Both grow on rocky slopes.

FIGURE 200. Thoroughwort
SCALE: 1 x 1¼

FIGURE 200. *Leaf detail*

FIGURE 200. *Flower detail*

201. **Longleaf brickellbush,** *B. longifolia,* is a much-branched shrub up to about 4 feet tall. Its stems are whitish, and its very narrow leaves may be from 1 to 4 inches long. Its numerous small greenish heads are from ¼ to ⅓ inch long. This grows in moist places such as along the Narrows Trail. Another species is *B. atractyloides,* a small, stiffly branched shrub with individual, many-flowered heads over ½ inch high, and ovate phyllaries. Its small leaves are strongly ribbed, ovate to lanceolate, and have a few small sharp teeth along the margins.

> B. Herbs (2 species of brickellbush are herbaceous but have been described with their shrubby relatives and should be looked for on p. 284).
>
> 1. Phyllaries white, papery (flowers everlasting-like); pappus of thread-like bristles.

Pearly everlasting, *Anaphalis margaritacea,* is a plant from 8 to about 30 inches tall. Its stems and the lower sides of the leaves are woolly white. Leaves are long, narrow and usually green on their upper surfaces. The heads are roundish, white and about ⅓ inch wide; the central flowers form a darker spot. It grows in open woods and has been found in Heaps Canyon but is rare in Zion National Park. **Cudweed,** *Gnaphalium wrightii,* is similar and more common. Its leaves are gray on both surfaces and are usually widest towards the outer end. Another similar **cudweed,** is *G. macounii.* They both grow on moist ground, often near springs. *G. palustre,* a shorter plant with its heads clustered and surrounded by more or less woolly bracts, is found on the cool high plateaus.

Pussytoes or **catspaw,** *Antennaria.* These plants have flower heads similar to those of the last groups, i.e. with white papery phyllaries, but the plants are much smaller. They have rosettes of silvery leaves and often form mats. There are smaller leaves on the upright stems. The male and female heads are on different plants and differ somewhat in appearance in the same species. In general these are plants of cool, wooded locations so are not to be looked for on the floor of Zion Canyon.

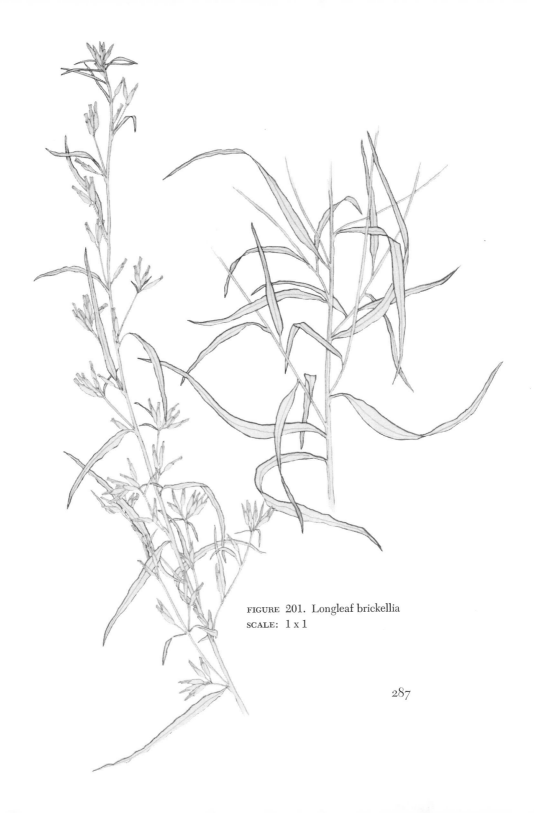

FIGURE 201. Longleaf brickellia

SCALE: 1 x 1

287

202. **Small-leaved pussytoes,** A. *parvifolia,* often has pink phyllaries. A. *neglecta* has stems up to 12 inches tall. Its phyllaries are usually white. A. *dimorpha* is a very low plant often not over 2 inches tall. It has only one flower head ⅓ to ½ inch high on each stem which has brownish phyllaries.

> 2. Phyllaries greenish, pappus of oblong, transparent scales.

203. **Douglas chaenactis,** *Chaenactis douglasii,* is a grayish plant with thick, pinnately divided leaves in a basal rosette and also a few along the stems. The flower heads are pinkish and held on erect branches. There are usually 10 pappus scales. *C. macrantha* with only 5 pappus scales also occurs in the Park.

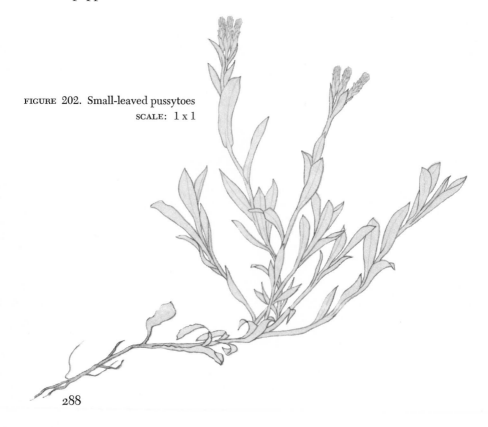

FIGURE 202. Small-leaved pussytoes
SCALE: 1 x 1

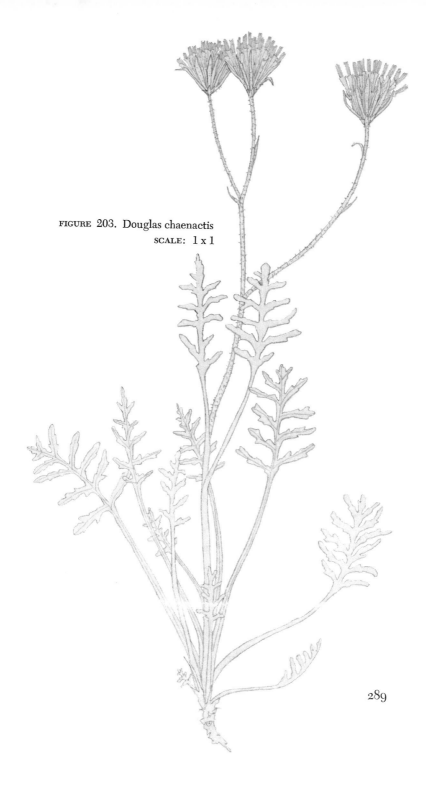

FIGURE 203. Douglas chaenactis
SCALE: 1 x 1

289

204. **Fineleaf hymenopappus,** *Hymenopappus filifolius eriopodus,* is somewhat similar, but its flowers are yellow. It has grayish, finely divided leaves. The base of the plant is woolly white. *H. filifolius lugens* is similar except that the leaves are green and mostly basal. The tops of the phyllaries are transparent and yellow.

C. Flowers in the heads all alike, but all are ray flowers with long, flat corollas (as in dandelions); stems and leaves have milky juice.

1. Flowers all yellow.

A. Leaves are in basal rosettes, rarely a few on lowest part of stem (dandelion relatives).

Agoseris (pronounced a gos′ eris) or **mountain dandelion,** *Agoseris.* These plants have their leaves nearly all basal, narrow and several inches long with some teeth or lobes. The achenes have long or short beaks to which the silky pappus threads are attached. Often there are dark markings on the phyllaries.

Orange agoseris, *A. aurantiaca,* has burnt orange flowers which turn pink or purplish as they age. The slender beak is about ½ as long as the body of the achene. This grows in moist meadows on the high plateaus. **Cutleaf agoseris,** *A. glauca laciniata,* has a short stout ribbed beak. It is quite common in open woods of the Upper Sonoran and Transition Zones. *A. retrorsa,* with the lobes of the leaves pointing backwards towards the base of the leaf, has achenes with slender beaks about 2 or more times as long as the body of the achene. It also occurs in open woods.

FIGURE 204. Fineleaf hymenopappus

205. *Microseris lindleyi* is similar in habit and appearance, but its pappus, instead of being thread-like, consists of 5 narrow shining scales from ⅓ to 1 inch long. These scales are 2-toothed at their tips, and between the teeth there is a slender bristle. The **common dandelion,** *Taraxacum officinale,* has long been naturalized in the Park.

206. *Glyptopleura setulosa* is a low annual desert plant with a compact rosette of finely pinnately lobed, white-margined basal leaves. Its flower heads are from 2 to 4 inches broad, pale yellow or almost white. It occurs in Coalpits Wash and other areas of the Lower Sonoran Zone. Its generic name is from two Greek words, *glyptos,* meaning "carved," and *pleura,* meaning "side," referring to markings on the sides of the achenes.

    B. At least a few leaves are along the stem, and usually there is a basal rosette as well.

    1. Corollas yellow.

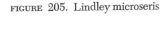

FIGURE 205. Lindley microseris

FIGURE 206. Glyptopleura

Hawksbeard, *Crepis intermedia,* is a much-branched plant with many yellow flower heads like small dandelions. Also its leaves resemble dandelion leaves. It grows in meadows on the plateaus. **Salsify** or **goatsbeard,** *Tragopogon dubius,* is a tall plant with long grass-like leaves. Its phyllaries are much longer than the lemon yellow corollas. Its stalks are inflated below the heads, and the achenes are long-beaked and tipped with plumed bristles. In fruit the head becomes an airy, glistening sphere 3 or 4 inches in diameter. **Meadow salsify,** *T. pratensis,* is similar except that its corollas are about the same length as the phyllaries. These are closely related to the cultivated plant called "vegetable oyster."

Wild lettuce, *Lactuca canadensis,* is a tall plant with thin green leaves about 6 inches long which clasp the stem. They are pinnately lobed, and the lobes are slightly curved backwards. The flower heads are yellow. This is a common plant of moist, shaded situations.

2. Corollas pink or white.

Milkpink, *Lygodesmia grandiflora,* is a green-stemmed plant with pink ray-like flowers in a head about 2 inches broad. Its few narrow phyllaries are nearly an inch long with narrow white margins. At the base of the involucre there are a few small bractlets. Leaves are very narrow and about 4 inches long. **Wirelettuce** or **rushpink,** *Stephanomeria* has flowers similar to milkpink only smaller. Its stems are green and its leaves inconspicuous. *S. tenuifolia* is a perennial plant with slender green stems from a woody crown. *S. exigua* and *S. pauciflora* have green much-branched stems and similar pink flower heads. **Desert dandelion,** *Malocothrix clevelandii,* is a slender, smooth, branched, annual plant with white or yellow flower heads and mostly basal leaves which have sharp teeth along their margins. The pappus consists of 1, or rarely 2, persistent bristles. **Desert chicory,** *Rafinesquia neomexicana,* has flower heads about 1½ inches broad with white corollas, sometimes streaked with pink or purple on the outside. It is a branched plant 8 to 10 inches tall with lance-shaped leaves which have narrow pinnate divisions. It grows in sandy areas on dry plains and mesas.

Most Common Non-Native Plants of Zion National Park

Goosefoot Family	*Chenopodiaceae*
*Lambsquarters	*Chenopodium album*
Poverty weed	*Monolepis nuttalliana*
*Russian thistle	*Salsola kali*
Amaranthus Family	*Amaranthaceae*
*Pigweed	*Amaranthus albus*
Purslane Family	*Portulacaceae*
*Common purslane	*Portulaca oleracea*
Buttercup Family	*Ranunculaceae*
*Bur-buttercup	*Ranunculus testiculatus*
Mustard Family	*Cruciferae*
Black mustard	*Brassica nigra*
Shepherds purse	*Capsella bursa-pastoris*
*Chorispora (80)	*Chorispora tenella*
Tansymustard	*Descurania obtusa*
Tansymustard	*D. pinnata*
Tansymustard	*D. richardsonii incisa*
Tansymustard	*D. sophia*
Clasping pepperweed	*Lepidium perfoliatum*

*Also mentioned in the text

Malcolmia	*Malcolmia africana*
Yellowcress	*Rorippa obtusa*
Tumblemustard	*Sisymbrium altissimum*
Pea Family	*Leguminosae*
Alfalfa	*Medicago sativa*
Black medick	*M. lupulina*
Red clover	*Trifolium pratense*
White clover	*T. repens*
Caltrop Family	*Zygophyllaceae*
*Puncture-vine	*Tribulus terrestris*
Paradise Tree Family	*Simaroubaceae*
*Ailanthus	*Ailanthus altissima*
Mallow Family	*Malvaceae*
*Cheeseweed	*Malva neglecta*
Morning-glory Family	*Convolvulaceae*
*Field bindweed	*Convulvulus arvensis*
Mint Family	*Labiatae*
*Motherwort	*Leonurus cardiaca*
*Horehound	*Marrubium vulgare*
*Dragonhead	*Moldavica parviflora*
*Molucca-balm	*Molucella laevis*
*Catnip	*Nepeta cataria*
Figwort Family	*Scrophulariaceae*
*Common mullein	*Verbascum thapsus*
Plantain Family	*Plantaginaceae*
*Common plantain	*Plantago major*
Lanceleaf plantain	*P. lanceolata*
Madder Family	*Rubiaceae*
*Catchweed bedstraw	*Galium aparine*
*Madder	*Rubia tinctorum*

Sunflower Family   *Compositae*
 Western ragweed   *Ambrosia psilostachya*
 Common chicory   *Cichorium intybus*
 Bursage   *Franseria acanthicarpa*
 Skeleton leaf bursage   *F. discolor*
 Prickly lettuce   *Lactuca scariola*
 Tarweed   *Madia glomerata*
 *Salsify   *Tragopogon dubius*
 Sowthistle   *Sonchus asper*
 *Common dandelion   *Taraxacum officinalis*
 Cocklebur   *Xanthium strumarium*

Common Roadside Flowers by Season and Color

SPRING

RED: In late March comes the **early Indian paintbrush** (161) as clumps of brilliant crimson "brushes" growing on stony hillsides, especially along the Watchman Trail and in the Oak Creek area. Later it will be found farther up the main canyon and in the side canyons. Its season lasts for several weeks. Then comes the **slickrock paintbrush** (162). This plant has shorter stems and more narrowly divided leaves. It often grows in sandstone crevices and is common along the upper trails, especially the East Rim Trail. In April look for the orange-red **monkey flower** (164) on dripping cliffs and the wet banks below them. This has opposite leaves and a 2-lipped corolla. With it and blooming at the same time is the **cliff columbine** (60).

One of Zion's most beautiful flowers is the **Utah penstemon** (167) with rich red, velvety flowers along an upright stalk. Its leaves are a pale blue-green. It will be seen first along the south-facing slopes of the Emerald Pools Trail, later in Oak Creek Canyon, and on west-facing slopes above the Zion Canyon Scenic Drive. In May **Eaton penstemon** (168) with tubular red flowers and dark rusty-green leaves becomes prominent. **Wyoming paintbrush** (163) with narrow leaves and sparsely flowered stalks begins blooming in late spring and continues, here and there, until autumn. Its green, long-pointed corollas protrude from the orange-red calyx and bracts.

298

RED-PURPLE, PURPLE and BLUE: One of the earliest plants with bright purple blossoms common on slopes and along trails is the **Zion milk-vetch** (103), a member of the pea family. Its leaves are pinnately compound, grayish-green and clustered. There are several other kinds of milkvetch with similar flowers. A larger flowered plant which somewhat resembles this is **Zion sweetpea** (101). A 3-petaled blue flower with bright orange anthers is **spiderwort** (22). It has very long narrow leaves. A 5-petaled bright or pale blue flower at the end of a slender stalk which is thickly set with narrow inch-long leaves is **Lewis flax** (108).

There are several kinds of **penstemon** (169, 170) with blue or purplish flowers and opposite leaves. These have snapdragon-like blossoms with irregular 2-lipped corollas. **Bluedicks** (28) are clusters of small funnel-form flowers at the tips of long leafless stalks. The leaves are long and narrow and all from the base of the stalk.

YELLOW: **Wild parsley** (132) is one of the earliest yellow flowers. It has shiny dark-green, fern-like leaves which at first lie flat against the ground. The tiny crowded flowers soon turn to brownish orange. Later this will have large, flattened, ribbed seeds. **Creeping hollygrape** (67), another early one, has compound leaves of 5 to 7 holly-like leaflets. This is an evergreen creeper and is widely distributed, usually in semi-shade, often under oaks. **Puccoon** (151) is a showy plant found on rocky slopes in the Park. Its creamy yellow flowers have long slender tubes which flare into 5 slightly fringed points. **Wallflower** (70) is a plant with clusters of 4-petaled yellow or deep orange blossoms found throughout the Park. **Desert marigold** (180) occurs on rocky slopes.

WHITE or PALE PINK: The very earliest flower to bloom in Zion National Park is the **sand buttercup** (63) with bluish, fern-like leaves. Its petals are usually white inside and pink or reddish outside, and the sepals are often red. It occurs in sandy areas on the East Zion Plateau. A mat-forming, early blooming plant with white or pink flowers is the **desert phlox** (142) which may be found in many semi-shaded situations in Zion Canyon and on the plateaus. **Prickly phlox** is a slightly bushy plant with pure white flowers and sharp-tipped leaves. It is often found in rock crevices. In early summer the **Palmer penstemon** (166) becomes conspicuous. It is a stout plant with tall stems bearing numerous fat, pinkish, snapdragon-like flowers and paired leaves which are joined around the stem. **Evening-primroses** (125, 126) with 4-petaled flowers are commonly seen in evening and morning along roadsides. The white petals turn pink as they wither in bright sunlight. The big white flaring cups of **sacred datura** (159) begin to appear in June and continue throughout the summer. There are few flowers in bloom in the canyon during the hottest part of the season, late June to mid-September.

AUTUMN

YELLOW: In September along the Scenic Drive yellow dominates the scene in all degrees from cream to orange. The large rounded bushes 2 to 5 feet tall, with plume-like branches crowded with deep yellow flowers are **big rabbitbrush** (198). They line the roadsides, climb the slopes, sometimes lean against rocks or grow on them. The low-growing plant close to the roadside with bright yellow daisy-like flowers and rough, grayish foliage is **goldenaster** (181). This is also along trails and interspersed among larger plants.

In partial shade and in slightly moist situations, on banks and along trails and roads, the tall **broom groundsel** (186) is abundant. Its slender stalks, 1 to 2 feet tall, often bend under the large, brilliant flower clusters of 2-toned yellow heads. Individually these flowers are about 1 inch across with bright yellow rays and orange centers. A low rounded bush covered with tiny yellow heads is **broomweed** (188).

PURPLE and LAVENDER: Asters are next in order of abundance and showiness. The bright purple one lining the roads in many places, and often making beautiful displays where it intermingles with groundsel on slopes and banks is **tansy-aster** (192). It has dark green, narrow, slightly toothed, roughish leaves. The centers of these flower heads are yellow but often turn to burnt orange as the flowers age. The pale lavender-flowered **glaucous aster** (191) with light blue-green leaves oc-
300

curs in patches on banks. In a few places along roads or among rocks you might see, in late afternoon or early morning, the red-purple or magenta, funnel-shaped flowers, set among dark, smooth leaves, of **Colorado four-o'clock** (52).

RED: The orange-red, funnel-shaped flower found at the base of dry cliffs and in some other rocky places is **hummingbird trumpet** (130). It catches the eye as a little flame might. On shaded, wet banks, under dripping cliffs and along little streams the **cardinal flower** (177) appears at this time of year. Its fringed corolla is deep crimson. Several flowers are borne on stalks 10 to 20 inches tall. Occasionally you might notice the few, last, orange-red flowers of the **Wyoming paintbrush** (163), a straggling plant at this season which has been in bloom since early summer. A rare red flower seen on ledges and among rocks on the plateaus is **Bridges penstemon,** a partially shrubby plant with 2-lipped corollas.

WHITE: The big flaring cups of **sacred datura** (159), white or tinged with lavender, are conspicuous in the morning. Also in the mornings and evenings the common **white evening-primrose** (125) is often seen. Its flowers have 4 distinct petals which turn pink as they wither. The **white-flowered Siskiyou aster** (190), about 15 to 24 inches tall, may be found in moist places.

Glossary

Achene. A hard, dry, small, one-seeded, non-splitting fruit

Annual. A plant which completes its life cycle in one year

Anther. The pollen-bearing part of the stamen

Appressed. Lying flat against another part

Axil. The upper angle between a leaf and the stem

Banner. The large upper petal in an irregular corolla, especially in members of the pea family

Biennial. A plant which forms only vegetative parts during its first season, produces flowers and fruits in the second season, and then dies

Bilateral. Used in reference to symmetry when a corolla may be divided into only 2 exactly similar portions

Blade. The flat, expanded portion of a petal or leaf

Bracts. Specialized leaf-like structures without stalks, often found below or surrounding flowers

Bractlet. A small, secondary bract

Capsule. A dry seedpod which splits when mature

Catkin. A scaly spike of small flowers which drops off. A pussy willow is a good example

Calyx. The outer circle of perianth segments, made up of sepals, either separate or united

Claw. The narrowed base of some petals

Convolute. Rolled up longitudinally with one edge inside the other

Corymb. A flat or convex flower cluster with branches arising from different levels. See ill. p. 317

Deciduous. Used of leaves which fall off at the end of one season of growth, or of petals or sepals which fall early

Decumbent. Lying down but with the tips ascending

Disk. In the composite family the central part of the head bearing tubular flowers

Disk flower. The regular tubular flowers on the heads of members of the composite, or sunflower, family

Divided. I have used this term for any depth of division not better described by toothed or lobed

Endemic. Confined to a limited geographic area

Entire. Describes a smooth margin, without teeth. See ill. p. 309

Exserted. Extending beyond surrounding parts

Family. A group of plants made up of closely related genera

Florets. The individual flowers in the composite and grass families

Funnel-form. Shaped like a funnel

Genus. A group of closely related species. The plural is *genera*

Glabrous. A smooth surface, without any hairiness

Glandular. Bearing glands which produce a stickiness on the surface

Glaucous. Smooth but covered with a waxy powder (bloom) which rubs off and which gives a bluish or whitish color

Habitat. The situation in which a plant grows

Head. An inflorescence in which many small stemless flowers are crowded together on a receptacle

Herb. A plant with no persistent woody stem above ground. Its stems die back to the ground each year

Herbaceous. Having the texture of foliage. Opposed to woody

Imperfect. A flower which lacks either stamens or pistil

Incised. Cut rather deeply and sharply

Inferior. Referring to the position of the ovary when it is located below the other flower parts

Inflorescence. The flowering part of a plant and the pattern of its arrangement. See ill. p. 317

Involucre. A set of bracts around a flower, umbel or head. See ill. p. 318

Irregular. Describes a flower in which the petals or sepals are not all alike; not radially symmetrical

Keel. The lower two more or less united petals in the flower of the legume family, which have a boat-like structure

Lanceolate. Used to describe leaves or other parts which are broader at base and taper to a long point. See ill. p. 313

Margin. The edge of a leaf or petal

Naturalized. Introduced from a foreign country but growing wild and propagating freely by seed

Nodding. Hanging down

Node. The joint of a stem. The point of attachment of a leaf or leaves

Nutlets. Applied to any small, hard, dry fruit or seed, with thicker walls than an achene

Obovate. Shaped like a section through an egg, but attached at the smaller end. See ill. p. 313

Ovate. Shaped like a section through an egg, but attached at the large end. See ill. p. 313

Pappus. The modified calyx in the composite family made up of hairs, bristles or scales and attached to the top of the achene

Parasitic. Growing as a parasite on another living plant

Pedicel. The stalk of an individual flower in a cluster

Peduncle. A flower stalk whether of a single flower or of a flower cluster

Perennial. Lasting from year to year

Perfect. Used of a flower which has both stamens and pistil

Perianth. The petals and sepals collectively, especially when they cannot be distinguished

Petiole. A leaf stalk. See ill. p. 308

Phyllaries. Specialized bracts which form the involucre of a composite flower head

Pistil. The seed-producing or female element of a flower

Pollen. Pollen grains, contained in the anthers; the male element in flowering plants which must be deposited on the stigma of the pistil in order that the ovules may be fertilized and develop into seeds

Pubescence. Hairiness on foliage

Raceme. An elongated inflorescence with several or more flowers attached by short stalks along a central axis. See ill. p. 316

Rachis. The axis of a spike or raceme, or of a compound leaf. Also the main axis of a fern leaf

Radial. Spreading from or arranged around a common center

Ray. Marginal flowers, especially those with strap-shaped corollas of the composite head. See ill. p. 318

Receptacle. The more or less enlarged top of a stalk to which other parts are attached

Reflexed. Abruptly bent or turned downward or backward

Regular. Flowers which are radially symmetrical. See ill. p. 315

Rootstock. An underground stem

Rotate. Wheel-shaped

Runner. A slender trailing stem rooting at the nodes or end, thus starting new plants

Salver-form. A united corolla with a slender tube which abruptly flares into a spreading, circular rim which may be entire or lobed

Sessile. Attached directly by the base; not stalked, as a leaf without a petiole

Shrub. A perennial plant with several woody stems, smaller than a tree

Spatulate. Gradually narrowed downward from a rounded tip

Species. A group containing all the individuals of a particular kind of plant

Spike. A type of inflorescence where all the individual flowers are sessile on the axis

Spur. A hollow, sac-like or tubular extension of a petal or sepal, usually containing nectar

Stamen. The male element of the flower. It consists of a *filament* or stalk which bears the *anther* containing pollen.

Stellate. Star-shaped

Stigma. The receptive part of the pistil, on which the pollen germinates

Stipule. A small, usually leaf-like, appendage at each side of the base of a leaf petiole. Seee ill. p. 308

Striate. Marked with fine lines

Style. A part of the pistil which connects the stigma with the ovary. See ill. p. 313

Superior. Describes the position of the ovary when the other floral parts are attached at its base. See ill. p. 313

Taproot. A stout, perpendicular main root, giving off small branches

Tuber. A thickened, solid, and short underground stem

Umbel. A type of inflorescence where the individual stalks are all attached at one point, the summit of the main stalk, in an umbrella-like arrangement. See ill. p. 317

Whorl. A group of three or more similar leaves or flowers radiating from one node

Woody. Refers to stems which persist from year to year and become hard

Illustrations of Terms used to Describe Plants

The following numbers refer only to glossary illustrations

LEAVES

1. This is a *simple* leaf which is *pinnately veined* (feather-type). The leaf is made up of *blade*, 1a; *petiole*, or leaf stalk, 1b; *midrib*, which is a continuation of the petiole extending through the blade, 1c; and a pair of *stipules*, small leaf-like structures at the base of the petiole, 1d.

2. This is a simple leaf, but it is *palmately* (like a hand) *veined* and *lobed*. It has 3 main *lobes* and 2 smaller ones. Its *margin* (the edge) is *toothed*. It also has a petiole.

3. This is a simple leaf having *parallel veins;* its ribs, or veins, are parallel to its margin, 3a. It is *sessile,* i.e. it has no stalk, but the blade is attached directly to a stem or twig, 3b. Its shape is *ovate,* i.e. egg-shaped, and its *apex,* tip, is *acute,* i.e. sharp-pointed, 3c.

4. Here is a *pinnately lobed* leaf. It is a pinnately veined leaf which has the margin indented between some or all of the main veins.

5. Leaves may also be *needle-like,* as in the pine family.

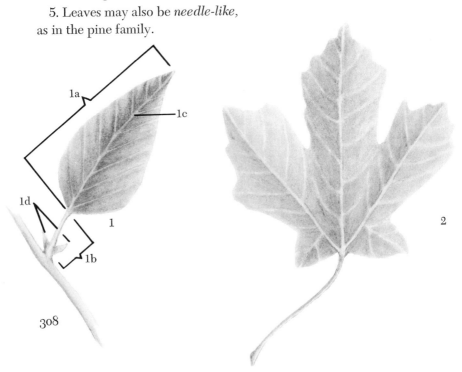

308

1

2

3c

3a

3

4

3b

5

6–7. When an individual leaf is made up of 2 or more distinct leaf-like parts, it is called a *compound leaf,* and each distinct part is called a *leaflet,* 6a, 7a. The best way to make sure if a leaf is compound is to see if there is a bud in the *axil* where the leaf is attached, 8a and 9a. Leaflets never have axillary buds, but there is always a bud at the base of a complete leaf. It is sometimes hard to see the axillary bud, especially in young growth. There are 2 types of compound leaves.

6. This is a *pinnately compound leaf.*

7. This is a *palmately compound leaf.*

LEAF ARRANGEMENT

8. These leaves are arranged *oppositely,* i.e. in pairs.

9. These leaves are arranged *alternately.*

10. If there are more than 2 leaves at one point on a stem, they are *whorled.*

TYPE OF BRANCHING

If the buds are opposite, as with opposite leaves, the branching is opposite, as in 8.

If they are alternate, the branching is alternate, as in 9.

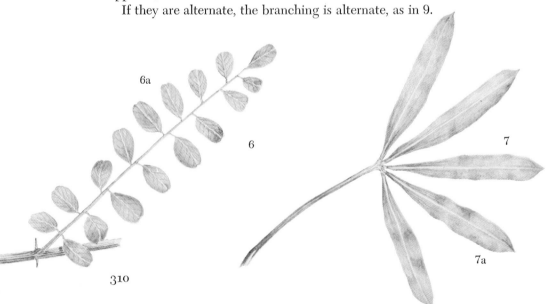

6a

6

7

7a

310

8a

8

9a

9

10

311

11. *Ovate,* egg-shaped and attached at the broad end, 11a.

Lanceolate or *lance-shaped,* broadest near the base narrowing to a pointed tip, 11b.

Oblong, tending to be rectangular with more or less parallel sides, 11c.

Obovate, like ovate but attached at the narrower end, 11d.

Oblanceolate, like lanceolate but attached at the narrower end, 11e.

Other descriptive terms used for leaves in this book are self-explanatory.

FLOWERS

The essential parts of a flower are the *pistil,* i.e., the female element, and the *stamens,* the male element.

The pistil consists of the *stigma,* which receives the pollen, and the *ovary,* which contains *ovules* which, after fertilization, develop into seeds. The stalk supporting the stigma and connecting it with the ovary is the *style.*

The stamen consists of the *anther,* which contains pollen, and a *filament* which supports the anther. A *perfect* flower must have both of these parts, but there are *imperfect* flowers where only one of these parts is present. The pistil, or pistils, and stamens may be in separate flowers or on separate plants. Other parts which may or may not be present are *sepals* and *petals.* The *sepals* collectively, separate or united, are the *calyx.* The petals collectively, separate or united, are the *corolla.*

12. This diagram shows a *complete perfect regular* flower with sepals, petals and stamens separate. One or more of the series of parts may be *united.*

13. This arrangement has the various parts attached separately beneath the *ovary* so the ovary is in a *superior* position. This is referred to as *hypogynous,* meaning "below the ovary."

11a

11d

11b

11e

11c

11

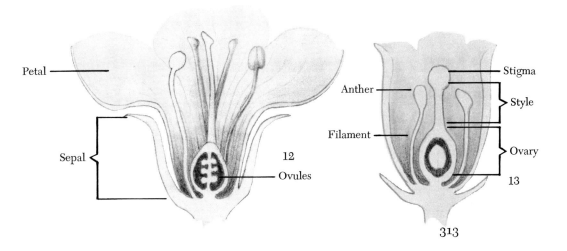

Petal

Sepal

12

Ovules

Anther

Stigma

Style

Filament

Ovary

13

3¹3

14. In this arrangement the flower parts are attached to the edge of a saucer, cup or tube formed by the base of a united calyx. It is said to be *perigynous*, meaning "around the ovary."

15. Here the ovary is completely enclosed in the calyx tube; the other flower parts sit on top of it, and the ovary is described as *inferior*. It is referred to as *epigynous*, meaning "upon the ovary." In some cases the ovary may be only partly inferior, i.e. more or less embedded in the calyx tube.

Flowers may be *regular*, i.e. radially symmetrical, as in 16 and 18. Or they may be *irregular*, i.e. bilaterally symmetrical, as in 17 and 19.

16. Here is a *regular* flower with *corolla* of 4 separate petals; 16a shows a separate petal flower; 16b shows a petal with a *claw*.

17. Here is an *irregular corolla* of *separate petals*.

18. This shows a *regular flower* with *united corolla*.

19. This shows an *irregular flower* with *united corolla*.

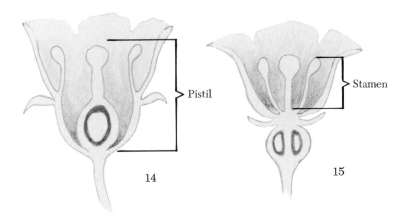

Pistil

Stamen

14

15

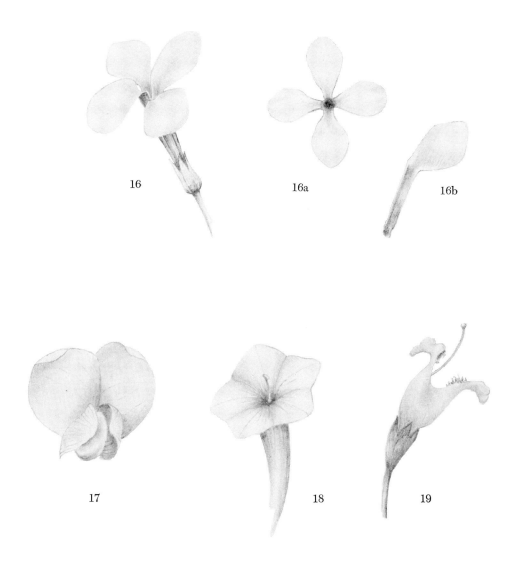

16   16a   16b

17   18   19

The part of the plant which bears the flowers is called the *inflorescence*. There are definite patterns in these arrangements, and each distinct pattern has a name. This character is useful in identification. The patterns referred to in this book are illustrated below.

20. A *raceme* is an arrangement where each flower is attached to a long, central stalk by individual stalks.

21. When flowers are attached directly to a long, central stalk with no individual stalks, it is called a *spike*.

22. A *panicle* is an arrangement where flowers are irregularly distributed on branches of the inflorescence, forming a loose cluster.

23. When each flower has its own stalk and all these stalks originate at one point, as in the ribs of an umbrella, the arrangement is called an *umbel*. Umbels may be flat-topped, curved or ball-shaped.

24. When each flower has its own stalk and each stalk originates at a separate place on the main stalk, but together they produce a more or less flat-topped arrangement, the result is a *corymb*.

25. When stemless, individual flowers are closely crowded together on the enlarged end of the main stalk, the inflorescence is called a *head*. The enlarged top of the stalk is the *receptacle*. Examples are clover or sunflower heads.

20   21

316

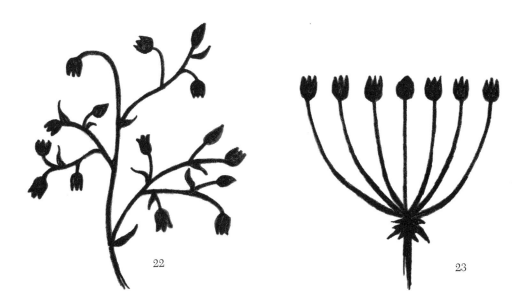

22

23

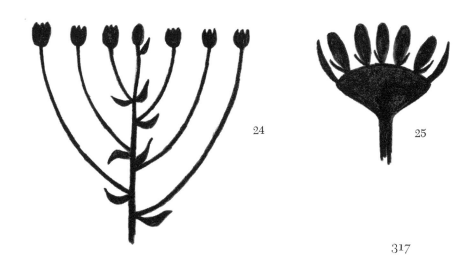

24

25

317

Flowers of the composite family are always arranged in the head type of inflorescence. Their parts are always attached to a receptacle. Because there are so many plants of this family, both in kind and in numbers, the kinds may be roughly grouped according to the type of flower head.

26. This is a long section through a typical head of the *radiate* group. 26a shows an individual *ray flower,* and 26b shows an individual *disk flower.* The *involucre* is made up of *bracts,* small leaf-like structures called *phyllaries* or, sometimes, *involucral bracts.* The involucres are more or less distinctive for different genera in the family.

27–30. Four different types of involucres are shown here.

For more detailed information on this important family, see p. 250.

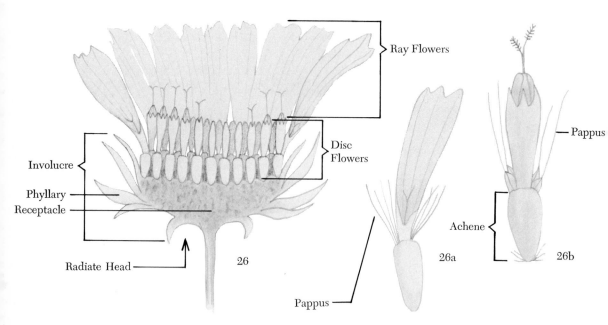

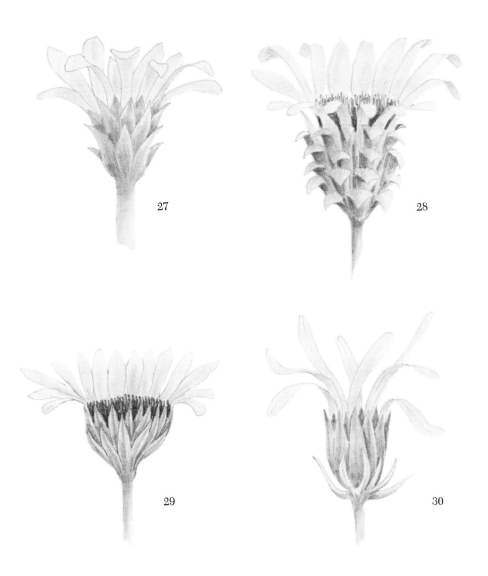

DIFFERENT TYPES OF INVOLUCRES

References

BUCHANAN, HAYLE. *Living Color. Wildflower Communities of Bryce Canyon and Cedar Breaks*. With color photographs by J. L. Crawford and H. Morris Buhanan. Bryce Canyon Natural History Association, Bryce Canyon, Utah. 1974.

CRONQUIST, ARTHUR, ARTHUR H. HOLMGREN, NOEL H. HOLMGREN, and JAMES L. REVEAL. *Intermountain Flora, Vascular Plants of the Intermountain West, U.S.A*. Vol. I, Hafner Publishing Company, Inc., New York and London. 1972.

HARRINGTON, H. D. *Manual of the Plants of Colorado*. Sage Books, Denver. 1954. Second edition. 1964.

HOLMGREN, ARTHUR H., and JAMES R. REVEAL. *Checklist of the Vascular Plants of the Intermountain Region*. U.S. Forest Research Paper Int. 32. 1966. This is the authority for the botanical arrangement and names for this publication.

KEARNEY, THOMAS H., ROBERT H. PEEBLES, and others. *Arizona Flora*, Second Edition. University of California Press, Berkeley. 1964.

NELSON, RUTH A. *Handbook of Rocky Mountain Plants*. Dale Stuart King, Publisher, Tucson. 1969.

RICKETT, HAROLD WM., and others. *Wild Flowers of the United States*. New York Botanical Gardens, McGraw-Hill Publishing Company. Vol. IV. *The Southwestern States*. 1970.

321

Vol. VI. *The Central Mountains and Plains.* 1973.

These volumes contain excellent color reproductions of many of the plants described in this book.

TIDESTRUM, IVAR. *Flora of Utah and Nevada.* U.S. Herbarium Contr. Vol. 25. Government Printing Office, Washington, D.C. 1925.

WELSH, STANLEY L., MICHAEL TRESHOW, and GLEN MOORE. *Common Utah Plants.* Brigham Young University Press, Provo. 1965.

WELSH, STANLEY L. *Flowers of the Canyon Country.* With color photographs by Bill Ratcliffe. Brigham Young University Press, Provo. 1971.

Acknowledgments

THE MOST HELPFUL BOOKS for wildflower study in Zion National Park and southwestern Utah are listed under References, p. 321. However, no one of them deals specifically with the area covered in this book, and so it was necessary to consult botanists and herbaria of the region. Much assistance was given by the individuals and institutions mentioned below, and I express my sincere appreciation to each of those named and to others unnamed.

To Arthur H. Holmgren, Curator of the herbariaum of Utah State University, goes special gratitude for the use of the herbarium, for help in determination of species, and for his painstaking reading of the entire manuscript. Also to both Dr. Holmgren and his wife, my sincere thanks for their personal kindnesses to me during the time I spent on their campus.

Others have given freely of their time and facilities: Mrs. Lois Arnow, the Garrett Herbarium of the University of Utah; Stanley Welsh, the herbarium of Brigham Young University; Wesley Niles, the herbarium of the University of Nevada at Las Vegas; John and Charlotte Reeder, Rocky Mountain Herbarium, University of Wyoming; William A. Weber, the herbarium of the University of Colorado; and all the helpful associates and assistants at these institutions.

To other botanists, particularly specialists in certain plant groups, I am indebted for determinations of critical species and for helpful sug-

323

gestions: Oscar F. Clark, University of Redlands, identification of some grasses; Robert E. Combs, Dixie College, St. George, Utah; Arthur Cronquist, New York Botanic Garden, species of the genus *Erigeron;* David D. Dunn, University of Missouri, some species of *Lupinus;* George J. Goodman, University of Oklahoma, some species in the *Polygonaceae;* and James L. Reveal, University of Maryland, help with the genus *Eriogonum.*

Special appreciation is due members of the National Park Service who have cooperated and assisted in many ways. Robert C. Foster, who as former Chief Park Naturalist of Zion National Park and Executive Secretary of the Zion Natural History Association first suggested the project, made the original arrangements, and has given valuable advice and encouragement throughout the four years it has been in progress. I am very grateful to him. The former Park Superintendent, Robert I. Kerr, the present Park Superintendent, Robert C. Heyder, the Chief Park Naturalist, Victor L. Jackson, the former Assistant Chief Park Naturalist, William M. Herr, and the present Assistant Chief Park Naturalist, J. L. Crawford, have all been helpful in giving encouragement and assistance. Jean Bullard, at the Rocky Mountain Regional Office of the National Park Service, edited the manuscript, gave helpful suggestions and corrected many typographical errors. I appreciate her help. Also I thank the members of the Board of the Zion Natural History Association for their interest and support.

In addition to the botanists and members of the National Park Service, there are other friends and associates who have been helpful, more of these than I can list, but I would mention particularly my close friend, Dee Koropp Godesiabois, who has been a valuable field assistant and has done much to promote this work. Alice Cherbeneau did a careful and professional job of editing in addition to typing the entire work. The photographers also deserve more than formal credit. Finally, my warm appreciation goes to Tom Blaue, who has been patient and skillful in making the many drawings.

Index

(numbers in parentheses refer to illustrations)

Park trails	Starting point	Round trip (km/mi)	Ascent (m/ft)	Round trip (avg. hours)	Remarks
Gateway to The Narrows	Temple of Sinawava	3.2/2	17/57	2	Easy, no steep grades. All-weather trail. Fine view of river flood plain. Trailside exhibit near Temple of Sinawava.
Weeping Rock	Weeping Rock parking area	0.8/0.5	30/98	½	Easy, surfaced, self-guiding trail. Water drips from overhanging cliff; springs issue from it. Hanging gardens; travertine deposits.
Emerald Pools	Zion Lodge or Grotto picnic area	3.2/2	21/69	2	Cross river on footbridges. Small pool formed by two falls. Loop or one-way trail.
Canyon Overlook	Parking area, upper end of large tunnel	1.6/1	50/163	1	A self-guiding trail. Mostly easy walking to top of Great Arch. Excellent view of Pine Creek Canyon and west side of Zion Canyon.
East Rim	Weeping Rock parking area	11.3/7	655/2148	5	Fairly strenuous foot and horse trail. Carry water, lunch. Cross footbridge and climb to East Rim Trail sign.
Hidden Canyon	Weeping Rock parking area	3.2/2	259/850	4	Fairly strenuous. Hidden Canyon represents Zion's "Shangri-la," an almost inaccessible canyon of quietness and solitude.
West Rim	Grotto picnic area	20.1/12.5	936/3070	8	Strenuous foot and horse trail. Carry water, lunch. Cross river on footbridge.
Angels Landing	Grotto picnic area	8/5	453/1488	4	Strenuous foot trail; experienced hikers only; steep climb. Half of trail hard-surfaced. Cross footbridge over river. Excellent view of Zion Canyon.
Watchman Viewpoint	River bridge above South Campground	3.2/2	112/368	2	View of The Watchman, Springdale, and Zion and Oak Creek Canyons. Changing vegetation.
Sand Bench	Court of the Patriarchs	5.5/3.4	152/500	3	Good view down canyon, and also of the Three Patriarchs. Horses.
Kolob Arch	Lee Pass	19.3/12	213/699 descent	8	Fairly strenuous foot and horse trail. Carry water, lunch.

Paved Road . . . . ━━━━

Gravel, Dirt Road . . . . ━ ━ ━ ━

Self-guiding Nature Trail . . . . 🧗

Amphitheater . . . . 📢

Ranger Station . . . . 🏠

Trail . . . . ━ ━

Parking . . . . ⬤

Picnic Area . . . . ⛱

Lodging . . . . 🍴

Campground . . . . △

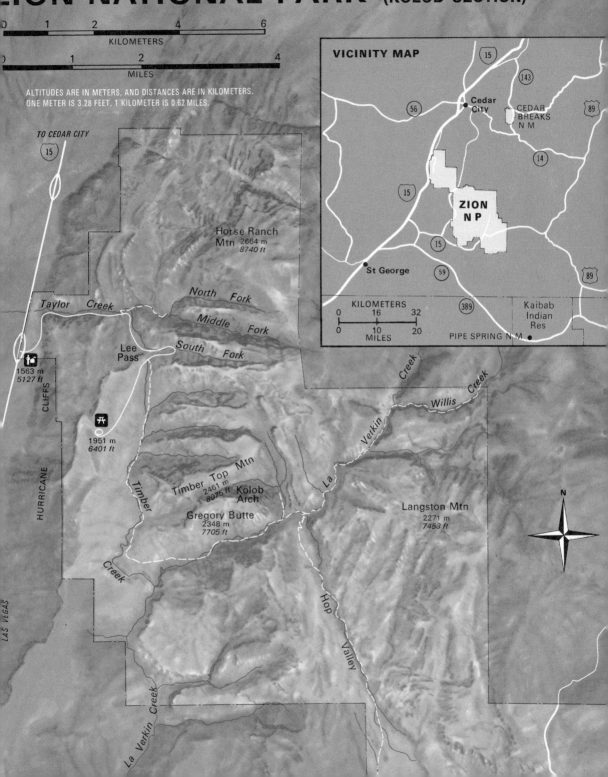

IION NATIONAL PARK (KOLOB SECTION)

0 1 2 4 6
KILOMETERS

0 1 2 4
MILES

ALTITUDES ARE IN METERS, AND DISTANCES ARE IN KILOMETERS.
ONE METER IS 3.28 FEET, 1 KILOMETER IS 0.62 MILES.

TO CEDAR CITY
15

Taylor   Creek

Horse Ranch
Mtn 2664 m
8740 ft

North   Fork

Middle   Fork

Lee
Pass   South   Fork

1563 m
5127 ft

CLIFFS

1951 m
6401 ft

HURRICANE

Timber

Timber Top Mtn
2461 m
8075 ft   Kolob
Arch
Gregory Butte
2348 m
7705 ft

Creek

La Verkin   Creek

Willis   Creek

Langston Mtn
2271 m
7453 ft

N

LAS VEGAS

La Verkin Creek

Hop

Valley

VICINITY MAP

15

143

56   Cedar
City

CEDAR
BREAKS
N M   89

14

15

ZION
N P

15

89

St George   59

KILOMETERS
0   16   32
0   10   20
MILES

389

Kaibab
Indian
Res

PIPE SPRING N M